Raising Confident Boys

100 Tips for Parents and Teachers

Elizabeth Hartley-Brewer

DA CAPO PRESS

A Member of the Perseus Books Group

DEDICATION
For my son, Stephen, and his constant friends Danny, Jonny, Pete, Dave,
Greg, Richard and Paul, with whom he has shared so much for so long

North American edition © 2001 Da Capo Press

Text copyright © 2000 by Elizabeth Hartley-Brewer

First published in the United Kingdom in 2000 by Vermillion,
an imprint of Ebury Press

Cataloging-in-Publication Data for this book is available
from the Library of Congress

ISBN 1-55561-320-9

Da Capo Press is a member of the Perseus Books Group.
Find us on the World Wide Web at http://www.dacapopress.com

Da Capo Press books are available at special discounts for bulk purchases in
the United States by corporations, institutions, and other organizations.
For more information please contact the Special Markets Department at
Perseus Books Group, 11 Cambridge Center, Cambridge, MA 02142 or
email jmccrary@perseusbooks.com

First Printing, March 2001

DHAD   04 05 15 14 13

Contents

Acknowledgments

As someone, clearly, with no direct experience of being male, I've had to check things out with a number of boys and male friends and colleagues. I've also had help from teachers who work closely with boys—and girls—at the educational frontier to give them meaning, respect and personal fulfillment.

I would like, then, to thank Dexter Hutt, Principal of Ninestiles School in Birmingham, and Gary Wilson, Head of English at Newsome High, Huddersfield, both of whom gave precious time to conversations and manuscript reading, not to forget their children who had to do without their attention at these times. I would also like to thank Geoff Evans, of the C'mon Everybody project; George Hosking, who works with young violent men to help them understand and calm their souls; Adrienne Katz, who founded the research organization Young Voice, through which growing boys and girls have been able to speak and be heard; Dr. Sebastian Kraemer for his paper, "The Fragile Male," and for responding so promptly to my e-mails; and Joanne Edelman, friend and mother of two boisterous growing boys.

The idea for this book came from Jacqueline Burns, my editor. Had she not been such fun to work with, I would not have written it. I am very grateful to her, for I have learned much in the process. Finally, I thank my son, Stephen. It has been a real privilege to be his mother. I wish him every happiness as he leaves his teens and embarks on adulthood.

CHAPTER 1

Understanding His Challenges and Opportunities

Boys are in the news as having a hard time at the moment. They seem to be struggling, finding it harder and harder to succeed, conform and find a comfortable role in life. Statistics tell us that boys experience more behavioral problems; get involved in more crime and at a younger age; are losing the academic edge they once held over girls; and demonstrate their despair in significantly higher suicide rates than girls. Social, economic and even educational changes seem to be undermining their essential manhood, and some see the future as promising little but constant pressure or failure, or both. Their self-esteem and motivation appear to be at rock bottom.

However, many boys continue to do exceptionally well and enjoy greater freedom, having thrown off the chains of only one vision of masculinity. They thrive on the challenge of living in this new world and find comfort in the permission to think, feel and act in tune with the warm heart within them.

Boys are lovable, amusing, destructive, proud and defiant. They come in all possible shapes and sizes. Evidence is mounting that their brains as well as their bodies are different from girls'. It matters a lot how they grow up and how much respect society and families give them. It really matters, too, that they don't see education as an all-female province. It is crucial that they are allowed to respond to their male instincts within an understanding environment, so that they may feel true to themselves without following images of manhood that will lead them into trouble. Boys need just as much love, care and attention as girls in order to become lovable, loving, resilient and well-rounded adults who can make the most of life. Boys' positive self-confidence must derive not only from being happy to be male and having a clear idea of what manhood means, but also from a secure sense of who they are.

Boys are half our future. Given the changes taking place in society, particularly in employment and the family, growing boys will naturally feel confused and uncertain about the future. For instance, what does fatherhood mean? How important are commitment and marriage? How should they manage their sometimes contradictory feelings of sadness, anger, tenderness, competitiveness and protectiveness? Yet, while these changes may be disturbing, they are also potentially liberating, for they offer boys more ways of being themselves and therefore more ways to strengthen their self-confidence.

In the future, parents and teachers may need to give boys more support and guidance as they navigate their way around the increasing choices facing them. Instead of being able to slip effortlessly into a preset stereotype, boys must look to what lies inside them and experiment with ways to express and develop the threads of self that are woven into the fabric of character. As self-knowledge increases, self-confidence deepens.

Boys now stand at a crossroad. They can choose a path leading to diminishing opportunities and greater self-doubt, or one toward self-development and deeper self-worth. Which route they choose will depend on the quality of their self-esteem.

When a boy has a good relationship with an adult who makes him feel understood, valued and wanted; when he feels supported so that he does well in school, becomes competent and confident; and, through his various interests, gains several reliable groups of friends with whom he learns to socialize and work out differences, he learns to face the future with confidence and courage. It is vital for his mental health that he avoids becoming isolated and sullen, for a world without others easily becomes peopled by personal demons.

Industrial buildings that house hazardous chemicals carry a warning sign on their walls. Parents should take equal heed when they see their son carrying a label with the three "I's": "Isolation," "Insecurity" and "Insignificance." These I's are explosive and create an emotional cocktail that can damage someone for a lifetime.

Internal strength is the antidote for these corrosives. In the past, boys had to toughen up emotionally and physically. Partly for survival on the battlefield, skins were thickened and upper lips stiffened, often through bullying, to condition men to hide feelings that could let their country down. Resilience is, undoubtedly, important, but boys—and girls too—also need to be flexible, to be able to regenerate themselves after setbacks, and to develop what we might call "emotional courage."

This does not mean denying feelings—far from it. Those who survive in the twenty-first century will have equipped themselves with sophisticated social and relationship skills. They will possess "emotional literacy," to use a current popular phrase. Boys must learn how to be in touch with their own and others' feelings and perceptions because technological progress and greater global competition are creating jobs that require creative teamwork, collective problem-solving, constant communication and joint approaches to risk.

Parents and educators of boys today are challenged to present them with a comfortable male identity without the Teflon armor that cuts them off from themselves and others. The nonstick, nonchalant world of macho culture gets males nowhere. Feelings and people should stick. By helping boys develop inner strength and by nurturing their sometimes fragile self-esteem, we can help them to become happy, warm, generous, confident individuals, fathers and contributors to our society in the future—to everyone's benefit, including their own.

CHAPTER 2

Meeting His Needs

It is hard to accept that babies start off not knowing what sex they are. They experience themselves simply in terms of their most basic needs. Gender awareness starts at about the age of two, and boys' essential needs are the same as everyone else's. Some people consider boys who show they have these basic needs to be "soft" like girls. They wean boys from needing something from others in case this undermines their capacity to be strong, independent and male.

Yet boys do need. On top of being fed and clothed, all boys need emotional sustenance: to be loved, cherished, appreciated, valued, noticed, admired, understood and accepted. When his needs are left unmet, a boy feels ignored and separate. He may conclude that there's something wrong with him and lose self-esteem. A boy who gets into drugs, crime or violence is possibly reacting, angrily and resentfully, against adults who stopped recognizing and meeting his needs before he was ready to become emotionally self-sufficient (if any of us ever are).

1   Boys need love, too

Boys often seek love in roundabout ways from parents and other adults close to them. When they are old enough to make sense of what it means to be male, they may decide this means feeling love but not being soft enough to show it or want it.

It can be hard for a boy to accept that being boisterous, and sometimes difficult and destructive, works comfortably with also needing to lose oneself in the warmth and safety of a hug. This may be even harder for older boys, particularly if the arms are female. So boys often use more aggressive tactics to get the love they need than do girls, who have far less emotional distance to travel to claim their emotional birthright.

If he's just jumped on you from behind or given you a painful punch, this can mean that he needs your love, so it is better to respond affectionately than to lash out. Your goal should be to reduce the parental ties gradually without leaving him feeling emotionally stranded and abandoned.

Parents

Teachers

• Beware of thinking, "I didn't get or need demonstrations of love, so he'll be the same." He is different, and those who "don't get" can turn this into "don't need" to hide sadness.

• If you feel strange giving him hugs, ask before and after if it is all right for you to do so.

• Blow kisses if kissing him feels intrusive.

• You can show love by sitting close while watching TV or reading, for example, or sitting on his bed at night.

• You can show love by being interested in his ideas, paying attention to and doing things with him, and understanding his feelings

• Teachers will not feel parental love for the boys in their class; however, they can make it clear that they enjoy, approve of and accept them.

• Giving special tasks to certain boys who lack confidence can make them feel significant, noticed, reliable and trustworthy.

2   Show that you understand him

He came home from school one day in a worse mood than I'd seen for ages. He was rude and flippant. He used words that sounded like playground talk. Then I realized he was probably repeating what had been said to him. He flung his arms around me and cried with relief that I had understood.

All children find being misunderstood extremely frustrating. It starts as an irritation, but when the mistake persists, a boy will begin to question whether his version of himself is normal, reasonable and justified. When boys see their wishes as continuously ignored or misinterpreted, they feel not only humiliated but also increasingly resentful, angry and, most damaging, self-doubting.

You can show understanding by anticipating his needs and—carefully—expressing his possible thoughts. You can say things such as "I guess you're feeling left out. Am I right?" This gives him room to disagree, and keeps you from coming across as infuriatingly all-knowing—and possibly wrong.

Parents

- Accept how he sees the world. He doesn't have to agree with you, nor you with him.

- Value his uniqueness. Tell him what you like about him.

- Look behind his behavior for possible causes and feelings. Let him know that you understand.

- Repeat what he says to you, to check that you've understood: "So you want me to stay in tonight because you're fed up with my working late so much this week, is that right?"

- Remember his likes and dislikes.

- State what he's likely to feel about something: "You're not going to like this, but I don't want you staying out all night."

Teachers

- Make a conscious effort to notice patterns in a boy's work that enable you to see him as an individual: "You really like painting birds, don't you?" or "You're always writing about fishing; it must be your passion!"

- Encourage classwork that shows boys' likes and dislikes. Try to remember a few for each student.

- For particularly trying boys, list four reasons why this might be so (excluding "difficult personality").

- Use "reflective listening" phrases: "What I hear you saying is that you did not feel you knew enough to begin this homework. Let's start from what you're sure you know."

3 Approve of who he is, even if you hate what he does

Every boy needs to be accepted and approved for who he is, not just because he has been "good" or "successful" and lived up to your ideal of who he should be. If he constantly tries to fill a mold you created, he'll quickly lose his shape and identity and find it hard to be sure who he is.

Young boys probably get told off more than girls. They are often more boisterous and noisy. They are more prone to accidents because they're less coordinated. They are less able to explain themselves because their language develops later. Clumsy reprimands convey disapproval and can do great damage. If you have to tell him off for these things, separate the person from his actions. This will leave his self-worth intact while he learns to control his behavior and understand its consequences.

A boisterous boy is often fit and fun as well as tiring. Don't lose faith in him just because you are unhappy about a particular act or attitude. Don't ever make him feel devastated by your criticism.

Parents

- Think about his good points before you comment on his behavior, to help you think positively.

- Avoid using the words "good" or "bad" about your son's behavior, because he'll take them as reflections of himself. Instead, describe what it is you approve or disapprove of.

- Saying "Right now, I see your behavior as . . ." also limits your disapproval to the moment.

- Hitting him with your hand or an object can damage him beyond repair and make him feel you completely dislike him.

Teachers

- Identify something you like in each student. Then it's easier to say with honesty that it's his behavior that's the problem, not the boy himself.

- Describe in detail the behavior that is outside the rules and avoid "You" statements: Saying, "I'm irritated by the way you are tapping your ruler" is less personally offensive and provocative than "You are being really irritating!"

4   Give plenty of praise

Children love to be praised. It is one of the joys of living and working with them to see them beam with pride and pleasure when they do something well and we notice. Children love to please those they care about.

Praise thrills boys because they need it, but it also teaches them self-discipline. Through praise and encouragement, boys get clear, positive messages about how they should lead their lives—what it is they should do—instead of only hearing about what they should *not* be doing.

Many people, especially men, find it hard to give praise, particularly to boys. Criticizing and blaming make them feel in charge and all-knowing. Praising, on the other hand, can make them believe they've lost that powerful edge, which feels dangerous. Some don't know what to praise or what words to use. Others believe praise will make a boy big-headed, lazy or oversatisfied with work that isn't perfect. But being noticed and appreciated usually makes boys try harder, and it teaches them to appreciate others, too.

Parents

- To show approval, you can say, "That's great," "Terrific," and "Good job!" "Thanks, that was really helpful" shows appreciation.

- Find something to praise, appreciate and notice every day.

- Boys can be praised for their thinking skills (choices, ideas, ability to solve problems), social skills (helpfulness, understanding, sharing and resolving conflicts) and physical skills (being good with scissors, at making things, at a sport), as well as for good work.

- Be specific: Praise what your son has done rather than go on in general about how wonderful he is.

- Praise the effort he's made more than the end product.

Teachers

- Encourage boys to judge their own work, not to rely on your view.

- Let them evaluate each other's work, so that praise doesn't always come from people in authority.

- Help them to feel proud of good work. Assume a boy is proud and say, "I bet you felt pretty happy with this piece of work when you finished it."

- Find something about them to praise every day, including their humor, sociability and creativity.

- For a boy who rejects all praise, showering him with it won't work. Select one thing you find truly pleasing and mention it three times every day for three weeks, so that he begins to believe and trust it is true.

5   Spend time with him

I know my dad loves me, but I barely know him. I know he works hard to support us, but we hardly ever talk. It makes me feel as if I am incomplete.

Survey after survey shows that children like to have their parents around, even if they're not actively doing anything with them. They like to see their fathers as much as their mothers, and boys need their parents' time as much as girls do. Even teenage boys want to see more of their parents.

Men and women work longer hours than ever before. This means that they spend less time at home with their families. Boys cannot feel loved and lovable, believed in and believable, respected and respectable, if the people on whom they depend seem not to care. Only if the important adults in a boy's life give him time and attention can he feel validated and develop any kind of self-worth. Meeting his need for stress-free time with you, when you focus solely on him, will help him feel confident and successful.

Parents

- Presents are no substitute for presence: Don't try to buy your way out of being with your son.

- When you're with him, put the answering machine on and spend time finding out what he thinks. Talk about what he has been doing and playing.

- Play with him. Join in or watch him doing his favorite activity, or say, "Come talk to me while I wash the car."

- If you don't live with your son, keep every promise you make to visit and stay in regular touch.

- Quiet time together can be as valuable as action-packed time.

- Try to do any work you need to do outside the office at home, so you're not cut off from your family.

Teachers

- Boys often act up to get attention. Don't let bad behavior be the only way they succeed in getting it.

- If a boy wants a conversation at an inconvenient moment, suggest another time when you can give him your undivided attention.

- Identify the quiet boys each week and organize with colleagues to make a special effort to speak to and engage with them daily in some way.

6 Talk with touch and words

Touch can reassure as well as relax. A boy who is never touched can feel ignored, ashamed and unworthy. His confusion about his need for the affirmation of affectionate touch may make him less confident about touching others as an adult, either with formal handshakes or in physical displays of affection with his own children and partners.

Touch can communicate better than words. It can say so much, in so many ways, and it is less open to misinterpretation. And it need only take a split second. The positive touch can be a full embrace or an arm around your son's shoulders. It can ask for nothing in return or seek a simple sign from him that he has acknowledged your gesture. It can demonstrate to him and to others that he belongs to you. It can heal an argument and say you're sorry. It can console him after a disappointment, show how proud you are or express equality and partnership. But touch can also hurt. Hitting is hurtful, and merely pushing your son away when you're angry can signal deep rejection.

Parents

- Little strokes of his forehead or hands at bedtime or while watching TV—or just sitting close—can be a way to introduce touch into your relationship.

- Experiment with little touches to replace words.

- If your son finds being touched uncomfortable or embarrassing, ask him what's OK and when.

- Consider buying him a pet to help him feel comfortable about expressing affection through touch.

- Ask your partner to massage, stroke or hug you as a reminder of how good it feels. This may make it easier for you to be more expressive with your son.

Teachers

- Child-protection issues make many teachers reluctant to touch children. In any case, as boys grow older, it becomes increasingly difficult and inappropriate to do so. Just standing close to a boy while looking over his work can show you accept him and feel no discomfort in his presence.

- Some teachers greet their class of young children individually as they enter the classroom, inviting each boy to choose how he wishes to say hello each time —with a smile, a handshake or nothing at all if that's how he feels that day.

7   Respect his right to know

Boys in particular like to live within rules and structure. They thrive when they feel secure and can predict what is going to happen to them. The unexpected can be disturbing. Sometimes things happen out of the blue and any adults involved can be equally surprised. But more often the adults know in advance and simply fail to keep a child informed.

Children need to be able to make sense of their world. If they can't, they live in social and emotional chaos. They make sense of their life both through the patterns that emerge when life is ordered and each day has a predictable shape to it and by being given explanations when there are changes. Young children's brains develop through constructing meaningful patterns, so every child needs to make sense of knowledge and events before he can learn.

When you explain things to your son, you show that you respect his right to know, empathize with his need to make sense of his world, respect his ability to comprehend and understand, and trust him with the information.

Parents

• Try to tell your son about things before they happen and as they happen. Afterward explain why something happened.

• You can tell him about your own feelings and discuss his.

• Tell him about changes in routines, partners and other relationships, and about absences.

• Tell him about your decisions and the reasons for them.

• You can give him facts, answering his questions about such things as death and divorce honestly, but in terms he can comfortably comprehend.

Teachers

• Give boys fair warning of any changes to the daily classroom routine.

• If you know that you're going to be away, tell your class in advance, and let them know who'll be taking your place.

• Explain why any punishment or consequence is being imposed.

• Explain specifically why a piece of work is either good or falls short of the required standard.

• Keep boys informed about the time it will take to grade important tests or projects, and explain any delay in returning work to them.

8 Boys do best when an involved man cares

Boys do well in all types of families, but they are more secure when a caring man is involved. This man may be a father, relative, neighbor, youth leader or someone from his school. We know from studies that the earlier this special relationship is established, the better; but otherwise the old saying "Better late then never" certainly applies.

Boys benefit from a special relationship with a father figure for three reasons: 1) Being with someone who obviously enjoys his company and is interested in what he does will give him faith in himself; 2) having a good relationship with a male mentor and positive role model will show him what he can become; and 3) the personal qualities of this person will enhance his understanding of people and extend his range of choices of how to behave.

Fathers can't always be this person, for various reasons. Try not to let jealousy stop somebody else you know from getting close to your son. Provided the relationship is a positive one, and you are sure there's nothing wrong going on, boys benefit from a reliable man giving them his full attention.

Parents

- A relationship with a father figure may start naturally, but if it doesn't, you could start by inviting a possible mentor out with you and your son. Or invite him over for lunch or to watch a video with you and your son.

- Identify your son's interests, and ask neighbors if they have similar likes or hobbies and could support your son with his.

- Don't put down someone who is showing an interest, or say hurtful things to your son such as "Why does he think you're so special?" You may think your son is a trial, but this won't be everyone's view.

Teachers

- Research shows that boys have been turned away from a life of crime or drugs by a teacher who showed a special interest in them and accepted them for who they were. Often the teacher was oblivious to his influence.

- Be aware of any individual's vulnerability and his need to be listened to and understood.

- Invite suitable men to participate in a range of appropriate class and school-based activities, keeping in mind that background checks are important.

- Explore the potential of local mentoring programs for vulnerable boys.

9 Be his last point of refuge

When life has been hard for your son, when he has had enough and no longer has the energy to be brave or keep up a front, he'll need somewhere to hide, somewhere and someone to be his last point of refuge. This is the place where he can be himself, and where—for a short time at least—no one is holding him accountable. Here he will feel accepted unconditionally. This is where he can truly relax, safe in the knowledge that someone is there for him who will take away his burdens when he can no longer carry them.

Home, for children, is the obvious place, and parents are the obvious people, because parents matter most to a child. However, there are times and situations when parents feel they don't have the emotional reserves to give their child the consolation he requires. When this happens, ask yourself whether your son wants any more than for you to be close to him, without saying or doing anything else. This may be all he needs.

Parents

- If he asks for forgiveness after getting into trouble, accept his olive branch and try to put the whole thing behind you.

- Giving him refuge does not mean you have to ignore difficult behavior forever.

- Take the waiting out of wanting: Anticipate his feelings and volunteer comfort when you can see that he needs it.

Teachers

- Boys can find it especially hard to admit mistakes and may get themselves into further trouble by offering multiple and increasingly thin excuses. Try to intervene and forgive before he digs himself in too deep.

- Some boys rely on school for their refuge, so make sure refuge is available.

- Help boys to be aware of the need for refuge through class discussion of whom they may go to and when, where and why.

- Peer counseling or mentorship programs can help boys feel more willing to seek refuge within school.

10 Make him feel he belongs

Human beings have a profound need to feel they belong somewhere and to someone. Your son's first need will be to feel loved by the two people who made him, but as he grows up, the more friends, groups and institutions he feels a bond with and can identify with, the deeper his sense of self will be. Fitting in somewhere says something about who he is and reassures him that there are others like him. Belonging to a family, a social or ethnic group, a club or school, or a place of worship also means that he is wanted, accepted and acceptable. It provides him with guidelines about who he is and how he should behave.

If a boy grows up without any sense of belonging to his family or school, if he feels rejected—for example, because of heavy criticism—he is likely to seek acceptance and a sense of membership elsewhere. He will seek groups of boys who have given up on trying to please and gain pleasure and status in unacceptable ways.

Parents

- Tell him family stories, so that he knows his and your roots.

- Include him in as many family events as possible.

- Understand how fashion and uniforms can be symbols of belonging, and help him to fit in—at a level that fits in with your family budget.

- Let him attend big school events such as dances, games and concerts so that he feels he belongs there.

- Be on the look-out for signs of aloneness. Suggest that he join a sports or social club or youth group if he spends a lot of time alone.

Teachers

- Circle discussions and similar arrangements can reinforce group identity and make each child feel like an equal member of the class.

- Stable groups allow a clear identity to form: Minimize staff and student changes and regroupings for boys who may be especially vulnerable.

- When there is a high turnover of students throughout the year, you must make constant efforts to re-establish the coherence of the class group.

11 Allow him some privacy

My mother wanted to know everything about me, especially how I thought about things. It drove me nuts and I felt sort of invaded. One day I screamed, "Stop trying to get inside my head!"

Having time and space just for yourself is part of growing up and becoming separate and independent. Growing boys need this, and parents should not get upset when their son tries to carve out territory that belongs exclusively to him or from which they are totally excluded. This territory might involve his body; it might be his bedroom; it might be his social life; it will very likely be his sex life. If he chooses to look at magazines in the privacy of his bedroom and you find out, do not broadcast this to family or friends.

Younger boys who feel the need for privacy may try to keep school and parents apart, not necessarily because they have something to hide—they just need some space.

Parents

- If school becomes his private space, try to give him more privacy elsewhere—in his head or in his room—so that he lets you in.

- Respect his need for some aspects of his life to belong to him alone. It's not a personal campaign against you.

- Some children who feel invaded or controlled by their parents will create a private world of their own that involves a lot of fantasy, to the point of habitually lying.

Teachers

- School is a crowded and public place in which both action and participation are valued highly. Boys whose home space is confined and similarly crowded may need to seek their privacy within school.

- Quiet rooms, or corners in classrooms, may help to meet this need.

- Boys who don't participate in certain lessons may be taking private time.

- Respect a boy's need for some time and space on his own.

12 Encourage a caring masculinity

Boys will be able to feel more at one with themselves and at ease with one another if they can develop their caring instincts in parallel with other features of their personality. Masculinity does not have to be identified solely with physicality, aggression, brutality, crudity or cruelty to the exclusion of other softer characteristics.

No one is suggesting that boys lose their gender identity to become like girls or that men ignore the effects of their hormones in order to imitate women. We all, women included, have a tough side and a tender side. Boys' self-confidence will rise when they don't have to deny important parts of themselves.

A recent survey estimated that five million workers are bullied each year, which represents a lot of misery. Of course, women can bully, too, but it is likely that more people in a position to bully will be men. When we fail to challenge young children's view of masculinity as associated only with power, aggression and control, the damage to individuals can be widespread.

Parents

• Give him permission to feel and express tenderness toward cuddly toys, babies, animals and his younger brothers and sisters.

• Teach him to care for other people.

• Try not to belittle any men you know or hear about who take on caring jobs or roles.

• Don't tolerate hurtful talk or behavior simply because you think "boys will be boys."

Teachers

• Encourage an all-school policy of zero-tolerance of macho talk that is based on violence, aggression or insensitivity.

• Avoid setting up community service as an alternative to sports. Playing a sport is not incompatible with spending time with elderly people.

• Ensure plenty of class discussion to raise awareness of and caring about gender issues.

13 Support him when he's stressed

Contrary to popular belief, stress is not something only adults suffer. In fact, children get a double dose, from events in their own lives, such as bullying, academic pressure and friendship problems, and from the added effect of adult stress, because we all behave less skillfully toward children when we're preoccupied with our own problems. Add to this the fear that a boy will have less experience of life and himself to trust that "normality" will resume, and we can see that he is likely to get more confused and disoriented than adults, not less.

Stressful events that can destabilize a boy are those that involve separations from those close to him and changes to his status and self-image or to the pattern of his life, in either routines or relationships.

Signs that he may be feeling distressed about something include a prolonged unhappy mood, becoming withdrawn, disturbed sleep, being very tired, being unusually thirsty, stomach and other pains, aggression, stealing, poor concentration and inattention, and becoming more clingy.

Parents

• Spend more time with him. Help to boost his self-confidence and ensure he gets plenty of sleep.

• Take him seriously, including his worries and his view of what he'd like to happen.

• Keep him informed of changes and decisions, so he feels more in control. Maintain regular routines to bolster his security.

• Giving emotional support to needy boys is tiring. Get more rest so you feel more able to give.

Teachers

• Brief yourself about and watch out for all the possible signs of distress in your students, including poor work, bad behavior, visits to the nurse and truancy. Respond accordingly.

• Try to find some time to talk to any boy who seems withdrawn and tired in class.

• Talk to colleagues and contact the boy's home if your worries continue.

• Be aware that your own stress levels may make you less tolerant of challenging behavior.

CHAPTER 3

Deepening His Self-Knowledge and Self-Awareness

Boys feel acutely the expectations of their families and society. The ideal man is supposed to be all-coping, all-powerful, all-knowing. To live up to this image, some boys feel they have to put up a front and deny not knowing all the answers, ignoring their natural sensitivity and instinctive aversion to wrongdoing. The more they follow this path, whether to protect themselves from ridicule or their parents from disappointment, the more boys cut themselves off from who they really are. As they do this, they in effect discard parts of themselves and create a dangerous void in which their feelings are so denied that they are unable to reflect on the causes and consequences of their actions.

The denial process can start early. How many parents, particularly fathers, feel comfortable with their young son wanting a light on at night, a pacifier beyond babyhood or someone to stay with him while he falls asleep? How many teachers taunt boys for shying away from catching a fast ball, getting a shot or dissecting an animal in biology? Boys need courage, but it should grow from inner self-confidence.

Our feelings make us who we are. When we are babies, our perceptions and passions give us our first sense of self. So we must take note of what pleases, frustrates, upsets or hurts us.

Knowing our feelings about things has practical relevance, too, for motivation and progress. In order to develop, boys have to know what they are capable of and what they need to learn before they can master a skill. Our ability to look inside ourselves enables us to have a sense of awe and wonder, and to appreciate beauty and understand others. Lasting intimate relationships depend on it.

Research shows that boys find it hard to evaluate themselves. Not only do they avoid doing it, they are frequently overconfident so they fail to prepare for exams and they underperform. When they fail, they explain it away by saying that everything will be fine if they try harder. Boys tend to cling to their inflated sense of self, which means they can't admit any weakness, let alone tolerate it. Parents don't help their sons if they demand flawless children.

Self-awareness promotes emotional literacy—the capacity to notice and respect other people's sensitivities. We understand others through understanding ourselves. Those who live and work with boys have a duty to help them develop their sense of self by stimulating self-knowledge.

14 Offer choices

Choice is all around us. It's great, because it gives us more control over our lives. Common sense tells us that children should also have choices, but how much, when and, just as important, why?

In a world of multiple choices, boys need to be able to make informed and responsible decisions. Your son will do this better if he understands his own preferences, is sure enough about them to resist outside pressure and can think through the consequences of his choices on himself and others. These thinking and reflective skills should be developed whenever possible.

Choice is important because it offers scope for self-determination. It enables a boy to feel he has some control over his life and that he is not powerless and controlled by others: Docility is not a useful quality for the future. Choice also helps to sharpen his sense of himself because it makes him consider what he really wants.

Parents

- Younger children can be given some choice about what or how much they want to eat or drink, what they wear, what they play, whom they play with and what story they hear or read at bedtime.

- Avoid suggesting that they go out and play with someone. Allow them to come up with ideas and playmates for themselves.

- Older boys can have some choice about when and where they do their homework, what (but not how much) TV they watch, what they spend their pocket money on and so on.

Teachers

- Respect a student's decisions: Don't ask him what he wants, then ignore his reply.

- Choices help to manage behavior in the classroom. For example, say, "You can stop talking and goofing off or you can have detention. It's your choice."

15 Manage choices

In larger families, meeting everyone's whims and wishes is usually impossible. It isn't good for children or for parents, either. Too much choice can undermine a boy's sense of self: If he never makes true choices, he won't discover what he really likes best. He can also become confused and unhappy if he has too many choices about too many things, because he won't feel that his parents are in charge and family rules will be blurred.

Too much choice can easily lead to arguments, since he won't realize when his demands go too far. In addition, it allows him to control and manipulate situations; it doesn't prepare him to cope with disappointment; it may encourage him to become selfish and insensitive to other people's needs; and it can take responsibility from him because he can always say, "Sorry, wrong choice—I'll try this instead," if he doesn't like the consequences of his initial decision.

To help a boy strengthen and deepen his self-confidence, the choices available to him must be both limited and managed.

Parents

- Managed choice means either/or decisions. You put limits on the choices, having already decided what you are happy to agree to.

- Limited choice means offering these choices only a few times a day.

- Avoid open-ended choices. For example, on a cold day, it's better to say, "Would you like to wear your jeans or your sweats today?" in case he chooses shorts. And don't offer more than three choices for breakfast.

- Make sure the choices you offer are realistic.

- Boys should not normally be in charge of how the whole family spends its time.

Teachers

- Choice is motivating: Boys who are given some choice about what they do and how they do it are often more committed to their work.

- Offer choice within project work—not too much or it becomes too hard to start, but enough to foster individuality.

- When there is little scope for choice in classwork, try choice-based activities, such as "If I could be a tree/food/color /musical instrument/car/ country/piece of furniture /an animal, I'd be a . . . because . . ."

16 Don't impose your views on him

My father was impossible. He couldn't discuss anything. He just stated his view and declared all others to be uninformed and stupid. He tried to tell me what to think and how to do everything. When I needed to survive on my own, I found it hard to get his voice out my head.

It's easy to become so convinced by your own status and wisdom as a parent or adult that you assert your own opinions, issue unilateral declarations and impose your own decisions almost without realizing it, squashing your son's growing need to discover where he stands.

Too much criticism or praise, or the extensive use of rewards, can have the same result: You are asking your son to live exclusively by your views and values, giving no space for his own to take shape. There has to be a balance. Children, particularly during adolescence when they deconstruct themselves before they reconstruct, often explore their new identity by rejecting any parental model. They should be free to cross that road without being run over.

Parents

- Seek his views: "I like it, but it's what you think that's important," not "That's great, don't you think?"; "What did you think of that TV show?" not "That was a load of garbage."

- Think carefully about the things you care about, and realize he is likely to target those as he breaks away. If he does, don't take it personally.

- With older boys, the more you push your views and values and assume they should share them, the more likely they are to reject them.

Teachers

- Encourage students to think ahead about what might happen next in, for example, a science experiment, rather than telling them what they should expect.

- Resist the temptation to deliver the standard arguments for and against something in classwork in order to save time. Ask your students for their views.

- If you get involved in working out a conflict between two boys, don't impose solutions on them. Encourage them to come up with their own.

- In general debates, however strongly you feel about an issue, keep your views to yourself and allow boys to explore theirs. This does not mean you cannot question and gently challenge.

17 Give his feelings space in your world

As a boy, I was forced to live on an emotional plateau—never allowed to express unbounded joy or the depths of sadness. Being checked by moderation in all things suffocated me and I almost lost myself. My own son jumps up and down when he's happy, and I love to see it.

How many times have people said to you, "You have no right to feel that"? Didn't it make you feel angry and small? Times have changed. We now understand that feelings are as important as thoughts in the development of our children as unique and giving human beings. If we reject our son's feelings, we reject him as he experiences himself.

Feelings used to be thought of as somehow inferior to thoughts, more closely associated with instinct and animals, something that governed human beings when we were primitive, not civilized and sophisticated. But feelings are often a rational response to a situation, and they can be crucial to survival.

Parents

• If you accept his feelings, he will learn to live with, manage and enjoy them also.

• Teach your son to ask for what he needs: For example, "I think you're feeling upset. Would a hug help?" can free him to volunteer, "I'm feeling upset and I need a hug."

• Accept his apologies and offer your own: "I snapped at you because I was upset about something that happened today. I'm sorry."

• It's fine to feel but not fine to hurt others because of how you feel. Jealousy, anger, frustration and resentment must be dealt with, not buried.

• Older boys often use music to explore and express feelings.

Teachers

• Give boys incomplete sentences to fill in, such as "'I'm happiest when . . .," "When I get angry, I . . .," "I feel most important when . . .," "I feel frustrated when . . .," "I tend to give up when . . ." and so on.

• Brainstorm anger: Invite your class to discuss how they feel and see anger. Suggest synonyms for it, such as powerlessness, rage, frustration and so on. Ask students to describe relevant situations and consider whether the feeling they describe fits any labels being discussed.

• Have each child write in a feelings journal, at set (and free) times, about their reactions to pieces of work, school or events.

18 Tell him his story

You took your first steps running away from the vacuum cleaner. It used to terrify you. One day, when it came close, you just took off!

Young boys love to be told stories about themselves—when they were babies, how older brothers and sisters reacted when they arrived and so on. These stories give your son a history. They are pieces of his life's jigsaw puzzle that he needs to complete his picture.

Older children like to hear other stories—about your childhood and school days, or the antics of their aunts and uncles. Such tales deepen your son's sense of belonging, as he learns more about what it is he belongs to. Each story will act as a connecting thread that will create a sense of continuity in him. Like a spider's web, the more linking threads there are, the stronger he will feel.

Talk about difficult times too. If you blank them out, it will not only break the thread and leave a gap in his history but also damage his confidence in the future.

Parent

• Get out family photos from time to time. Talk about the people and events shown in them. This can fill gaps in his understanding of family history, generate laughter, lead to further conversations, reinforce your son's identity and increase his confidence.

• Regularly recall past vacations, birthdays or treats that were fun and brought the family together.

• If you can, collect and keep for your son items such as favorite toys, books, clothes and first shoes, so that he may revisit the past and bring it to life.

• Talk about problems. Don't bury them. He has a right to information about himself.

Teachers

• Personal life-lines: In a group, discuss special experiences that have marked students' lives and what made them significant, how they felt at the time and so on. Ask each child to draw a vertical line on a large sheet of paper (the line represents their life from birth, at the bottom, to the present, at the top). Have them write their own personal positive and negative events on either side of the line.

• Not everyone has a happy family story to tell. Focus on good and bad, happy and sad experiences to ensure a full and realistic picture that leaves no one out.

19 Encourage reflection

Reflection means standing outside oneself, looking in at what has happened and asking questions such as why, how and what if? It means "to consult with oneself" and "to go back in thought." Reflection entails reliving your experiences and having a silent conversation with yourself to understand them and the connections between them. You get to know and understand yourself better through reflection. It helps you make sense of your life, but it is something that is difficult for many boys to do.

Encourage boys to reflect, because thinking backward is the first step to thinking forward, which is important for learning, keeping relationships, managing conflict without violence and planning one's life. If boys cannot reflect on their views and actions, assess the good and the bad and figure out what they might need to change, they will be unable to develop or make progress in anything. Becoming aware of how they feel and behave helps them to understand other people's feelings and behavior and, therefore, to anticipate any problems with others. Understanding their past helps them face the future.

Parents

- Recap and reflect on the day's events with your son each night as part of his bedtime routine. Invite him to think aloud about both good and bad aspects of it.

- Do it yourself, modeling phrases such as "I wonder if I could have done that another way?" and "I really felt excited/angry when it happened." Apologizing shows reflection in action.

- Read books with story lines to your son starting as early in his life as possible.

- Encourage imaginative play and dressing up.

Teachers

- Ensure that boys read fiction regularly as well as nonfiction. Discuss story lines and characters.

- Encourage many discussions about "what if" situations.

- Introduce role reversal in drama to explore alternative experiences.

- Ask boys to write down two negative descriptions of themselves on one piece of paper and two positive on another. Transfer them to a large board and ask, "Are you always irritating? When? Why?" and so on, to help them see their behavior is connected with specific situations, not who they are and always will be.

20 Arrange winding-down and quiet time

The typical boy is a bundle of energy who needs to let off steam and be on the go, but he also needs to be able to slow down when the situation or a person requires it and to feel comfortable within himself when he does stop. Activity is great, but children are more likely to explore their inner selves when they are quiet.

Quiet time means the chance to be calm, to wind down, to relax or even escape. Quiet time also means peaceful togetherness, being at rest and content to be alone. Each boy has his own way of unwinding. One will prefer to flop in front of the television; another will require the boundaries of a bath to contain him. Some choose to relax by kicking a ball; others will be happy to contemplate and reflect as they doodle.

Being quiet at such times gives a boy the chance to let his thoughts roam, to find out what is inside him and learn to be at peace with and within himself.

Parents

• Discover his mechanisms for winding down and encourage him to do it, especially after rough play and after school, when he can find it hard to "come down."

• Respect his need for his own quiet space, even if it is not in your home.

• Encourage quiet togetherness. Watch TV or a video together, make time for morning hugs in bed if he is still young, or drive him to his friends' houses once in a while.

Teachers

• Simple breathing and relaxation exercises can work well with grade school children. Older boys may need considerable encouragement to participate, but it's worth a try.

• Have a clear ending planned for lessons, especially those in which there has been a lot of activity. Use this time to recap and encourage students to reflect on what has been taught and learned.

21 Explain your thoughts and feelings

"Children need models more than they need critics," said the French philosopher Joubert. Boys will learn to identify and express their thoughts and feelings safely and comfortably if they see you do the same.

It is particularly important for boys to see their fathers or male role models being open about their emotions and giving serious thought to their ideas. One significant and unhelpful element of macho maleness is that opinions are asserted in a commanding and dictatorial fashion and presented as "the truth." This obliterates the possibility that others, including children, may see things differently.

Thoughts and arguments should be offered and explained, not asserted, with the possible exception of key matters of discipline. A useful principle is to assert your right to be heard, not your view of the world. Inner strength is based on tolerance and respect, not domination, and such a view is also liberating: If you don't need to dominate, you don't always need to be right.

Parents

• If you are angry, upset or frustrated, explain why. Don't just shout.

• When you explain your reactions to your son's actions, he learns to assess and anticipate the results of his behavior. This helps him to become responsible.

• Tell him how you arrive at decisions, by saying, for example, "I first thought this, then I realized that, so I decided . . ."

• You are responsible for your feelings. Say "I felt angry when . . ." not "You made me angry."

• If your son swears, ask him to find an alternative word to express what he's trying to say, and do the same yourself.

Teachers

• Help your students find the best language with which to express their thoughts and feelings.

• Try to express yourself as precisely as possible, too.

• Use "I" phrases in order to avoid generalized blaming of an individual student or group of students for anything.

• Emotional literacy requires an emotional vocabulary. Boys need to discover which words they can use to express their feelings. If you present their options well, they will enjoy widening their vocabularies to replace expletives.

22 Keep communicating

I thought my son was fine. He seemed to get on with his life, although he was alone a lot, and I got on with mine. We didn't talk much. Then in the middle of his final exams, he crashed. Now he won't work, go out or talk. We're in a real mess.

Children and adults who don't communicate can pay a very high price. Communication skills lie at the heart of social and emotional health and success, and a boy will not be as comfortable with talking if adults, especially parents, don't talk to him. No conversation implies no interest, which he is likely to interpret as neglect, so family silence can have a devastating impact on his self-esteem and his trust in future relationships.

But family conversation also helps a boy to be comfortable with expressing his views to other adults in positions of authority as well as among his own peers. It contributes to confidence and will help him to stand his ground when dealing with professionals and authorities in the future.

Parents

- Keep talking, even if it feels uncomfortable. The more you do it, the easier it will become.

- Try to eat together as often as possible. If it's only occasional, ignore his bad table manners and swallow hard if he challenges you about controversial subjects.

- If you want to take issue with something, start with the word "I": "I'm not happy with doing all the chores and I'd like some help."

- Always stop and listen.

- If you have to be away, for work or for pleasure, set aside time when you return to touch base with him again.

Teachers

- Never assume that withdrawn, silent students are fine, although they make your work as a teacher easier.

- Although quiet students may simply be taking time out, be alert to long-term patterns. Talk informally and socially to such students. Talk to colleagues about them. Step in sooner rather than later when necessary.

- Vary lesson plans and allow for small-group work to encourage involvement and participation.

- In all lessons, nurture the skills of communication: reflection, listening and tolerance.

23 Encourage self-assessment

Although our children love to know they have pleased us, what we should try to encourage from the start is the confidence to evaluate and praise themselves.

Boys seem to have particular trouble with self-criticism. When they do evaluate themselves, many are too cocky and give themselves more credit than is due. While this confidence can be a delight to see, it can be dangerous, leading to self-satisfaction, laziness, poor preparation and unrealistic expectations—not to mention wounded self-esteem because they know it's a front. Being a boy, facing the demands that he does, your son is just as likely to respond to a shattered ego with denial and pretense as with a resolve to improve.

Self-assessment is important because it is central to independent learning. Many boys find it uncomfortable because they dislike both the responsibility it places on them and admitting that they could have done better. But more experience of self-evaluation is the only way out of this problem. The sting is removed from criticism when it comes from themselves.

Parents

• Avoid doing all the judging so that your son won't become dependent on your opinion and lose faith in his own.

• When your son asks you what you think of something he has done—a painting, an essay, a sports achievement, a music piece—turn the question back to him. What matters, ultimately, is what he thinks of his effort. Getting him used to deciding for himself is crucial.

Teachers

• Encourage boys to assess each other's work, in pairs, as a first step to becoming honest about their own work.

• Boys in preschool and kindergarten work well with a "plan, do, then review" approach. Older boys can do this, too.

• At the end of any piece of work, require boys to say what grade they think it merits. Then you can explain why and how it did, or did not, meet the standards for that assessment.

• Once self-assessment becomes frequent and normal, there will be no excuse for boys being dangerously overoptimistic about their abilities.

24 Hear the sound of silence

During adolescence, our son became almost mute. He spent hours in his room and hardly spoke. I was frantic, but it was the same for a few of my friends, so gradually I relaxed about it. He got through it, of course, and since he started college, he's back to his old self.

This parent eventually trusted his instinct and things turned out OK, but take care. If your son withdraws and becomes more silent, you cannot necessarily assume that everything is normal, because it might not be. His behavior could be a sign of unhappiness and depression.

However, your son does not have to talk all the time. Silence can mean he feels comfortable and does not need to fill every moment with words. It can be understood as quiet togetherness. The important thing is not to ignore it when a boy becomes quiet. Hear the silence, reflect on it, accept it for a time and see if you can find out what he is doing with it. Step in if you believe he is withdrawn from others as well as yourself, and if there are other signs of problems.

Parents

• Keep talking to your son—about things that won't start an argument—but don't force him to respond.

• Suggest doing something together that doesn't rely on talking but that you can share, such as swimming, bowling or going to a football game.

• Watch out for signs of trouble or danger, such as your son leaving late for or missing school frequently, changes in his eating patterns, unusual smells that could indicate drug or alcohol use, and any drop in the standard of his personal grooming.

Teachers

• Small-group activities encourage participation and offer less chance to hide behind silence.

• A boy who clams up in the classroom may be afraid of making mistakes or be distracted by problems. It's important to find out why he does not talk.

• Try introducing activities that require every person to speak in turn.

CHAPTER 4

Giving Him a Positive View of Himself

To manage the change and uncertainty that will characterize the twenty-first century, boys need to learn to see themselves and their capabilities in a positive light. If your son is going to manage several career changes successfully, adapt to new situations and markets, sell himself as a self-employed consultant or skilled craftsman, or negotiate constructively within relationships, he must believe in himself and feel he has many talents to offer. If he grows up seeing himself as a source of pain, anger, disappointment and disaster, he won't have confidence to take on challenges or commitments.

So how can adults help to create boys who are motivated, enthusiastic and full of optimism? It is vital to be supportive, extend their horizons and give them plenty of positive feedback, but it is also essential that we cut down on blame, nagging and criticism. These send harmful messages about how likeable and competent our sons are, with damaging consequences for their emotional stability, self-esteem and motivation.

Not only sticks and stones hurt. We can appreciate that hurtful things said to a boy in the playground will wound him. It is far harder to acknowledge that our own constant criticism will make a boy feel there's something wrong with him and undermine his confidence, independence, initiative and morale. He will be looking over his shoulder all the time, hearing your voice, wondering which of his actions will be next in line for your disapproval. Shouting, unwarranted blame and harsh, erratic punishment have a similar effect—they shatter his security.

We find many ways to justify our negative words and excuse ourselves. We may believe he deserved it or knows we really love him, or see his challenging reactions as a sign that our words didn't hurt, not realizing the shield he raises is a protective fiction. Men, especially, may believe a boy needs toughening up if they sense he is easily hurt. But a boy who "can't take constructive criticism" has, in fact, taken a bucketful of it and should be given no more if he is to have any energy left to protect his self-respect.

Neglect hurts, too. Institutionalized teenage offenders consistently mention feeling neglected by parents who lead lives in which they hardly feature and who allow them too much freedom for their age, which they interpret as indifference. What counts to a boy is not his parents' declaration that he is loved, but whether they actively demonstrate this love to his satisfaction.

25 Understand his difference

Every boy is different. A boy can be adaptable, affectionate, funny, sensitive, quick to cry, find it hard to concentrate or to share, live in a fantasy world or be down-to-earth. He can be resilient, jealous, generous, imaginative, prefer noise or quiet, be neat or messy, seek company or choose solitude. He may feel, play, think, learn and enjoy things in a way that is different from other people. These characteristics define who he is as a human being, regardless of his gender. A boy will have a clearer picture of the different elements within himself if close adults put what they see into words.

To take the analogy of an artist's palette, the more "colors," or traits, utilized, the more varied and interesting the painting. Parents, and sometimes teachers, often see a boy as "naughty." If he is not "good" (which for those parents means never doing anything wrong), then he is automatically "naughty." In that situation, boys learn to see themselves as either all good or all bad and, if it's the latter, unsuccessful too.

Parents

- Fill in your son's "personality palette." Write down his likes and dislikes: what he likes to or won't eat; his favorite games, pastimes and activities; his clothing style; what he does well; places he likes to go; how he works best.

- Be positive: Traits you view as negative may be the reverse of positive ones. For example, he may stand up for himself with friends but be "too assertive" with you.

- Tell him what you see: "I really like the way you . . ." or "You're very sensitive, aren't you?"

Teachers

- Consult with other staff members to determine specific strengths and weaknesses of a student you find "difficult."

- Be aware of different learning styles (ask what students prefer) and vary lessons appropriately.

- Ask students to get into small groups. In each group, select one student and have the rest of the group bombard him with all the strengths and unique features they see in him (no negative comments are allowed). One person should record the contributions, listing ten to fifteen of his strengths.

26 Don't compare him to others

For some boys, living in the shadow of a brother or sister is a nightmare that stays with them for the rest of their lives. They can never quite shake off the humiliation and feeling of inferiority. Comments such as "Your brother would not have produced work like that" or "You're not as talented as your sister" can ruin pride and kill ambition. Friends, too, can be used (or rather abused) as a model for him to measure up to: "Why can't you do as well as John?" But far from acting as a spur, adults who suffered these taunts as children say their childhood was tainted by them.

Even handing out equal praise can be limiting. Saying, "Dan's the brainy one in the family and Jim's the athlete" may give each brother something to be proud of, but it will make it less likely that either will explore their potential in the other's field of interest. Brothers and sisters may be genuinely different, but they also make themselves different in order to create their own territory, and when skills become territories, children can become tribal.

Parents

• Every child responds—and is entitled to respond—differently to situations because each child is unique. Comparisons will undermine his self-confidence.

• Make it clear there is room for more than one artist, poet, pianist or tennis player in the family.

• Labeling causes resentment and may tempt a boy to do and become the opposite out of spite.

• Don't compare your son with how you were or what you did at his age. He is himself, not you.

Teachers

• Positively value each child as an individual. Never use references to siblings to disparage or coerce work.

• Be especially supportive of originality and creativity.

• The most useful comparison, if one is to be made, is self-referential: Compare each boy's current performance or piece of work with his last.

27 Respect his feelings

Feelings are fundamental. They make us who we are. Many parents have trouble accepting that their boys can be fearful and anxious. Men aren't supposed to have those vulnerabilities, and the sooner a boy overcomes them, the sooner his parents can be reassured that their son is going to be a "real" man. They also stop having to spend valuable time and energy dealing with those fears and feelings. Fear of the dark, water, spiders, losing friendships, failure, nightmares and bogeymen all seem irrational to parents and test their patience. They respond with rational arguments, but, for the boy, the fear may be purely emotional and, therefore, irrational.

Whether it is delight or disappointment, fear or fury, joy or jealousy, boys are entitled to have their feelings acknowledged and respected by their parents and caregivers, just as girls are.

Parents

• Respect his fears and anxieties.

• Share his delights and disappointments.

• Acknowledge and describe how he might be feeling, so that he develops a vocabulary that will help him understand his reactions.

• Jealousy is natural, normal and acceptable, but it's not acceptable to hurt anyone because of jealousy.

Teachers

• As part of a literacy strategy, give young children a feelings journal in which they can write how they felt about particular lessons, projects or homework.

• Fear of failure explains a wide variety of behavior that obstructs learning. Encourage boys to be open about fears.

• At all ages, drama and role-play can allow both boys and girls to explore emotions safely.

• Debates in mixed gender groups will enable boys to learn more about empathy.

• Encourage boys to explore emotions by reading literature.

28 Listen with both eyes

My dad doesn't really listen to me. I'd love him, one day, to put down his newspaper or turn off the TV when I'm talking to him. I feel like a nobody.

Listening involves looking just as much as hearing. When you listen with half an ear, it usually means you are concentrating on something else you are doing, not looking at your son. When you look at him, three things happen: 1) You have to stop what you're doing so that your full attention is directed at him; 2) eye contact with him helps you fix your thoughts on him and what he has to tell you; and 3) you are able to read his body language and facial expressions, which will help you to interpret any thoughts he may be unable or unwilling to express.

When parents and teachers don't listen well, or at all, they are conveying the message that they and their business are more important. Boys who are ignored will feel insignificant and undermined, and their self-esteem cannot possibly flourish.

Parents

• When your son wants to tell you something, use your eyes first, not your ears. Stop what you're doing and focus on him.

• Study his facial expressions. Look for any hidden meaning. Notice how he is standing or sitting, and his tone of voice.

• Let him know you are taking him seriously: "This sounds important. I think I'd better sit down and listen properly."

Teachers

• Show awareness: "My antennae tell me there is more to this story than you're saying."

• Teach students about body language and be vigilant about its application in all oral activities in the classroom.

• Provide plenty of opportunity in discussions, debates and presentations for boys to listen to and respect each other's contributions.

29 See with both ears

Like listening with both eyes, seeing with both ears means helping adults be more sensitive to boys and their experiences. A boy's inner world is as important to him as the outer, visible one. Certainly both influence the quality of his self-esteem, but the former is possibly more important.

You get a glimpse of what might be happening inside him from listening to his "self-talk"—that is, what he says about himself and how he says it. For example, a boy may seem to be doing fine at school, perhaps doing especially well on a particular test. You then feel you can relax and assume he feels good about himself. He may, however, respond to the result by saying, "That was a fluke. I didn't deserve it," or "I'll probably fail next time." His words show that, inside, he doubts himself. He may have plenty of friends, but if one backs out on doing something with him and he says, "He's probably got something better to do," it again indicates a tendency to put himself down.

Parents

Teachers

• Listen for, and rephrase, negative self-talk.

• Try to keep a record of what he says and how often he makes such comments, even if he seems to be kidding, to understand any pattern or the scale of the problem.

• Simply denying a child's self-criticism won't have much impact. Repeat often, over a period of time, that you see him differently: "I think you're quick to see the point, amusing and fun to be with . . ." or "I see you as someone who . . ."

• Be positive! Discourage negativity and challenge "I can't do this" assertions.

• Encourage self-evaluation tasks in which students write about their performance, highlighting the areas where they believe they performed best.

• If a boy says he's no good and knows nothing, draw a horizontal line with "knowing nothing" at one end and "knowing everything" at the other. Invite him to mark the spot that represents how much he really knows, and he'll realize that he does know something.

30 Respect his play

As a child, I had a great time, making up stories, making a little trouble, spending hours outside with my friends.

Boys are playful. They love to have fun with both friends and family. Play is essential to the development of self-esteem and confidence. Through play, boys find out who they are, because through the choices they make about what to play or do, whom to play with and so on, they gradually flesh out their self-concept and gain an identity, two essential prerequisites for acquiring self-esteem. Through play, boys also discover what they can do, because play develops verbal, social, manual, planning, problem-solving, negotiation and physical skills, which enhance their self-confidence and their ability to socialize and make friends.

Finally, through safely managed independent play, boys gradually realize that they can handle life on their own.

Parents

- Encourage your son to play with you, with his friends, on his own, indoors and outdoors.

- Let him choose what to play most of the time.

- Respect his play by giving him fair warning of when he must stop and by not spoiling his fantasies with teasing or ridicule.

- Pretending, putting on costumes, drawing and creative games are just as important for boys as for girls. They allow them to be spontaneous, creative and imaginative, all of which help them do well at school.

- Get involved in his computer games—computer skills are the way of the present and future.

Teachers

- Show respect for students' hobbies and interests. Utilize these for individual presentations and projects.

- Role-play and improvisation can be fun and can provide a great release for boys, giving quiet ones a more assertive role or more outgoing ones a smaller or quieter role.

- Though play is important, there are times when it is appropriate and times when it must stop. Winding-down time after recess and activities can help to mark boundaries.

- Respect younger boys' action play, because there is often more of a story line than there seems.

31 Let him impress you

Boys get a real boost when someone they admire shows they are impressed with them. They puff up with extra confidence and pleasure. It does their self-esteem a lot of good. Showing you are impressed is, of course, a form of praise, and a very effective and straightforward form of it.

Being impressed has little of the measured judgment implied in some other forms of praise. Most important, it is unconditional. "I am really impressed!" or "That was impressive!" says it all—no ifs and buts to qualify or detract from the message. There is nothing grudging about being impressed.

To say you are impressed also clears the air of competition. Some fathers, especially, feel they need to be stronger, better and more clever than their sons—and they must prove it. But being impressed doesn't mean a boy has "won" in some way or will stop trying. It simply shows admiration, which is what boys thirst for.

Parents

• Ask him to help you fix things, organize things, decide things, clean things, then say, "Wow, you're good at that, aren't you? I'm impressed!"

• Show you respect his skills and his views: "You're good at fixing things—can you help me with this?"

• Give him responsibilities so that he can test himself, develop his skills and feel trustworthy. Let him know that he has become responsible.

• Let little ones win in little ways, and show that you're impressed.

Teachers

• Give boys responsibilities: for example, reporting back from group discussions, looking up something that will benefit everyone's classwork. Show how impressed you are with the outcome.

• Begin questions in the classroom along the lines of "Ben, you know a lot about this . . ."

• For an impressive piece of work, gauge the appropriate method of reward, public or private.

32 Fight the might of muscles

The classic male body may be the dream of many, but not every boy is going to grow up naturally endowed with broad shoulders and rippling muscles. Many families, and some racial groups, simply don't transmit the right genes to bring this about. Boys may not worry about the pout of their lips, the look of their buttocks or the size of their eyes, but they experience as much anxiety about body shape and the condition of their skin as pubescent girls.

Muscles take on a special value wherever physical strength is prized above other attributes and where might is viewed as right. If everyone in your family respects social, rather than physical, qualities in human beings, and rejects the use of muscle power to end disputes, your son's self-esteem will flourish whatever his shape and size. Social and emotional strength matter far more in the long term. It is also important that he can admit freely when his body is sick and not working properly.

Parents

• Teach him to care for and honor his body, whatever its shape, by supporting him when he's sick and helping him stay clean, fit and healthy.

• Be careful what you say about men's physiques, so you don't applaud media stereotypes.

• If he wants to do weight-training, and it's safe, support him; don't tease. Make sure he knows that he's lovable as he is and that girls go for personality and humor more than looks.

• Don't teach him to hit back at or exploit physical size with other boys.

Teachers

• Avoid comments such as "You're big and strong; you can help me with these books."

• Make boys aware of the power of advertising in establishing preferred body images.

• Talk about what makes a "real man."

• Break down stereotypes through discussion, classroom displays and teaching materials.

• Initiate work on bullying and do not tolerate physical fights on or near school grounds.

33 Lead him when he's ready

My son just got into Harvard. You know, he didn't read well until he was seven; he just wasn't interested. I wasn't worried then, and now I know I was right.

Parents can't wait for their children to walk, get out of diapers, read, swim, ride a bike and so on, for many different reasons, some more honorable than others, but this eagerness can be counterproductive for a boy's self-confidence.

All children learn best when they are ready. "Ready" means not only that they're willing—hungry for the knowledge or skill—but also comfortable and confident enough to progress, instinctively aware that the necessary prior knowledge is in place, so they will be able to make sense of what they find.

When a boy can influence what he does and when, he begins to know himself intimately and to trust his judgment, to the long-term benefit of his self-esteem.

Parents

• "If it's Tuesday, it must be karate"—some boys are driven, literally and metaphorically, by their parents to attend a stream of afterschool activities, to keep them busy and give them opportunities to shine. But children get tired. Beware of forcing your son into extracurricular pursuits that he doesn't enjoy and at which he won't succeed.

• Avoid pushing him to progress too soon. If you push too hard, he may actually lose ground.

Teachers

• Encourage mastery learning, in which students are told what they are expected to learn, how they are expected to demonstrate their learning, how it will be assessed, and then are allowed to choose their own way to meet expectations. Such programs are particularly effective for weaker students.

• When a child is motivated, his work improves. Try to enhance each boy's motivation so that he may develop as he wishes to.

• Boys like to learn in and through groups. If a student seems stuck, try having him work in a group.

34 Accept his friends

We'd all been together through everything, for years. Mom always liked them. When we left school, she paid for us to go out and have a good time together to say thanks to them.

Friends are important to a boy, whatever his age. They make him feel he belongs, that he's liked and likeable. They validate him, share his needs and widen his interests. They help to give him an identity. He thinks: "I am friends with this type of person, so I am also like this." Friends help him to fill his time and have fun, to become sociable and learn to be part of a group. They make him more confident and provide the security of safety in numbers.

Real friends will offer support, empathy and loyalty, and be there when things go wrong. His friends will become part of him, which makes it doubly hard if you tell him he's made the wrong choice. Reject his friends and you reject him. When his friends "fit" your family, it gives you a warm feeling of pride and relief that he's accepted by others. It's far harder when children "get in with the wrong crowd," when his friends subvert your plans, challenge your values and cause problems.

Parents

• Invite his friends to your home or out with your family so that you can get to know them better.

• Tell your son what you like about his friends.

• Compliment your son on his ability to be a good friend to others.

• If his friends are a bad influence, get him to list what he's getting from them and consider whether his needs could be met in another way.

• Talk about what he expects from a real friend—and let him decide whether his friends have these qualities.

Teachers

• Although you should recognize and respect natural friendships, arrange classroom seating and the composition of groups for project work in ways that encourage mixing and minimize peer pressure, bullying and isolation.

• Explore the issue of friendships and peer pressure through school assemblies, personal and social situations, education and drama.

35 Enter his world carefully

My son became passionate about fishing after his uncle took him a couple of times. He wanted me to come too, but it took so long and I had the younger one, so I never did. I told myself I wanted to keep it as his thing and didn't want to muscle in, but when his passion dwindled, I realized how badly he'd wanted me to share in his interest. It was my fault that he gave up.

It can be hard to judge the amount of involvement a boy wants us to have in his life, especially when he is at an age when he needs to become more separate and independent. There can be no clear answers—we must simply remain sensitive to the issue and judge each situation as it arises. There are two useful principles to keep in mind: 1) Show interest, but don't be intrusive, and 2) remember that your prime role is to be his parent, not his friend. You can be effective and loving without being his best friend, who should come from his peer group.

Parents

- Show interest, but don't be intrusive.

- Share and show an interest in his hobbies but don't take them over. They don't have to become your passion, too.

- Give him the space and territory to be different and separate from you without cutting yourself off.

- Older boys frequently use music to explore and establish their new identity. Ask which bands he likes, but don't make them your favorites.

- Sporting events are safe to share. They bring different generations closer.

Teachers

- In any class discussions about personal and family matters, acknowledge your students' range of family types and personal experiences, but tread carefully in these areas.

- Plan ahead about how you would respond if a student ever became upset during discussions of personal issues.

36 Cut down on criticism

Jimmy was ten and doing well in school, to the delight of his parents. Then he overheard his mom chatting to a friend whose son was struggling. Jimmy's mom didn't want to upset her friend further by parading her own son's success, so she replied, when asked, "Oh, our Jimmy's no good at anything!" These few words had a devastating effect, destroying his confidence. He never trusted himself again and dropped out of college ten years later. Only then did Jimmy and his mom learn the truth from each other, but it was too late.

Adults are usually totally unaware of the destructive impact of their careless words, which can do untold damage. Even an offhand statement can destroy a future by allowing self-doubt to take root. Boys are as sensitive to criticism as girls. Constant harping and criticism lead to self-doubt and guilt about letting parents down. If a boy fails to please, he'll assume he disappoints. Eventually he'll feel totally useless and rejected, although he will probably hide it well.

Parents

• Focus on one behavior at a time and ignore the rest. Piling on criticism will make him resentful and uncooperative.

• Accentuate the positive: Say what you want done and trust him to do it. Choose a day when you comment only on the good things he does.

• Try to stop watching and judging, because this implies you are also controlling and mistrustful.

• Banish humiliating phrases such as, "I can't take you anywhere," "I wish you'd never been born," and "You make me sick."

Teachers

• Teachers' words can hurt as much as anybody's.

• Teasing, sarcasm, ridicule, shouting and blame are put-downs that hurt, shame, degrade, damage and humiliate. They sap motivation and morale and are never justified.

• It takes four "praises" to undo the harm of one destructive criticism.

• Turn your "don'ts" into "do's."

• Doubts are more cruel than the worst of truths. Keep a boy's self-doubt at bay.

CHAPTER 5

Demonstrating Care through Love and Rules

One five-year-old boy who had recently started school was asked what he liked best about it. Without hesitation, he replied, "Assembly, because that's when we get told what we can and can't do." His mother was very surprised, for he liked to have his own way at home. What she didn't see was how much comfort and security boys find in rules and structure.

One teacher I know believes that boys generally have a more fragile self-esteem than girls, except for those who have grown up with a high degree of consistency at home. These boys knew where they stood and what they could do, were secure enough to learn new things and were happy to take responsibility for themselves.

We show that we care in many different ways. The right kind of food makes him grow strong and healthy. Ensuring that he's clean and appropriately clothed keeps him warm and protected from disease and ill health. Having fun and sharing our lives with him make him feel emotionally secure, as does being understanding about the mistakes he will inevitably make as he gains skills, confidence and maturity.

Shortcuts don't work. Giving in to a boy because you can't be bothered to argue won't persuade him you care; neither will showering him with presents. Having guidelines for behavior that will protect him and others demonstrates your concern.

Positive discipline builds positive self-esteem. When there are clear guidelines for behavior and a daily routine, children can relax. They don't have to decide everything for themselves or worry about getting into trouble and, when they behave, life is not only calmer but filled with the warmth of other people's approval. When adults set limits and are sufficiently involved to monitor a boy's behavior, he realizes that they care.

Of course, rules must be fair and reasonable. The popular phrase "tough love" does not give adults the right to be brutal. Discipline without dictatorship and punishment without humiliation ensure that boys won't need to challenge perceived unfairness or face parents' put-downs that will eventually shatter their self-esteem. Also, boys thrive on the approval of a loving father or father figure. A boy will react defensively and distance himself from a harsh disciplinarian or indifferent father, the very person he needs to be close to.

By showing, through love and rules, that you care, you help him to care about himself and others, including you.

37 Love him for who he is

One of the hardest things to do is to love and accept boys for who they are. Instead, we dwell on what we see as their flaws and worry about our dreams for their future. We worry that our hopes might be dashed. But if you focus on an idealized future, the present will always disappoint. And if you let your disappointment show, the relationship that should fill your son with confidence will undermine him instead.

Boisterous boys are like bear cubs. They are rambunctious, full of energy, sometimes clumsy, and have an urge to explore, play and roughhouse. They are spontaneous, noisy, bubbly, irrepressible, with a capacity for both fun and fury, but they also have the capacity for deep and serious thought. Sensitive boys are calmer, more thoughtful and prefer to watch, test and experiment before they commit; but they are also capable of fun and spontaneity.

A boy may mistime the humor, mistake the signal, mishandle his strength or misjudge the moment, but his urge to react and assert himself must be understood and nurtured.

Parents

• Imagine your son has lost all the characteristics that irritate you: He cleans his room, takes his shoes off at the door, volunteers to wash up, never forgets anything. Be aware that if he becomes who you want him to be, his essential personality may have gone and he will have lost himself.

• List all of his pluses and minuses. Balance each negative characteristic with a positive one. Then add more pluses than minuses to the list.

• Let him live in the present, not with your fears. He has many years in which to grow and mature before adulthood.

Teachers

• If a student becomes a "clone," modeling himself on you or an ideal, he is likely to find it difficult to take risks and handle making mistakes.

• To help the younger child appreciate who he is, outline him while he lies on paper on the floor, then invite him to fill in his shape with his characteristics.

• Ask older children to list twenty things they like to do, beside which they should add the date when they last did them, a "$" beside things that cost more than five bucks, an "F" if they prefer to do it with a friend, an "A" if alone, a "P" if it needs planning and an "M/D" if a parent did it as a child. Then they can tell a story about their interests and likes.

38 Don't make approval conditional on good behavior

One of the things prospective employers are wary of when they interview people for jobs is any applicant who "brown noses," seeks approval, avoids disagreement and seems not to have faith in his own judgment. Anyone showing these signs is rejected because insecurity and uncertainty are unhelpful in the workplace.

Of course, we all have times when we feel insecure, but some people feel it more than others and some are hampered by self-doubt most of the time.

The tendency can start in childhood. Boys grow strong inside when they feel approved of, loved and accepted for who they are. If an adult's approval is conditional, forthcoming only when a boy is being "good," he will be forever looking over his shoulder, creating distance between his instincts and his actions. Always having to play to the parental audience, he will soon lose sight of himself and never develop any sense of personal integrity.

Parents

- Accept that he won't be perfect and that mistakes are not only inevitable but also important for learning.

- See the funny side of his errors.

- Behavior talks: He's not bad, just trying to say something. Look behind any naughty behavior for possible reasons.

- Disapprove of what he does, not who he is.

- With an older boy, you can disagree with what he wants to do, yet still support his right to do it.

Teachers

- Be aware that reward systems for work and behavior might lead unsuccessful boys to feel disapproved of.

- Show approval toward all students: Respect, show interest in and talk to each one, not just the accommodating and successful ones.

- Involve all students in decision-making, to develop their independence and self-esteem and to demonstrate that you trust and approve of their ability to make judgments.

- Show that you value a wide range of skills.

39 Hear his complaints

When my mom picked me up from grade school, she used to stand talking with her friends for ages. I was tired, wanted her and wanted to be home. One day, I told her this. She said she hadn't realized and she changed right away.

A very young child takes life as it comes; he knows no different and passes no judgment. But as his sense of self and his speech develop, he begins to reflect and see the world from his own perspective. He becomes aware of his own desires and wishes and can form his own judgments. That's when he starts seeing that things can, indeed, be different. When he puts this concept into words, he is expressing and risking his total experience of himself.

This is why as soon as he is able to voice, or display, disappointment or dissatisfaction, you should take his complaints seriously and respond respectfully. His self-confidence and self-understanding depend on it.

Parents

- Let him know that it's okay to complain: Put a sheet of paper in his bedroom for written comments if he has troubled facing you.

- Listen to his complaint—it could be his first step toward a compromise and an important lesson in conflict resolution.

- Try not to be defensive or competitive if he complains.

- Be ready to apologize if he says you have gone too far.

Teachers

- Turn any complaint into a question or statement: "It sounds like you think this grade isn't fair because you tried really hard this time, is that right?" or "I think I need to explain myself more completely. Thank you for letting me know."

- If you are able to enter a student's world, see how things are for him and accept his perspective, you will be modeling empathy and teaching him emotional literacy.

40 Acknowledge his disappointments

Disappointments are part of growing up. Boys have to learn that they can't always get their way, and that when they don't, life doesn't fall apart. We all have to learn to compromise, and sometimes to do without.

If any parent sets out to make sure their son never experiences disappointment, he or she will end up being enslaved to him. He will not learn to live with and through setbacks, and it will not help him understand himself, because he will never have to decide which of a range of alternatives is really important to him.

However, there are times when disappointments matter a lot, when they not only should be acknowledged but also avoided actively. If the people your son needs to rely on and trust let him down frequently, it can lead to a profound sadness that may develop into depression or other mental-health problems in later childhood or adulthood.

Parents

• Try to predict when your son might feel disappointed.

• Don't ignore or dismiss his sadness.

• Talk about it. Show insight and understanding by letting him know you know what he's going through: "I know you'll be disappointed, but we can't go bowling until next week. I know you were looking forward to it. I'm sorry it can't happen and that I raised your hopes."

• It could be dangerous if he often feels that you have let him down, rather than simply being disappointed when not allowed to have or do things.

Teachers

• Most boys will feel disappointed if they get a poor grade despite trying hard, though they may try to pretend otherwise.

• Try to acknowledge this when you give feedback, and if you think a student made a special effort, acknowledge this too. Tell him not to be discouraged and assert your confidence in his ability to learn.

• Give him hope. Discuss with him what he thinks needs to be done and what he can do differently. End the conversation with a summary of steps he can take to improve his performance.

41 Hold on to your authority

I thought I'd lost it. He wouldn't do anything I asked. I felt completely useless and became scared to try again in case I was ignored again. Then I realized that, just like his mother, I had all the authority I needed and I didn't need to prove it by shouting and screaming. I calmed down, thought ahead, decided on a few things I wanted him to do and stayed firm and fair. It worked, and we both feel so much better for it.

Adults have to find the right balance between staying in charge and getting caught up in power struggles. You can demonstrate authority in many quiet ways. Making firm decisions about your family's or class's routine, or what behavior is right for your family, is one way. Being unflappable and showing trust that boys will cooperate as asked or expected is another. When you take clear responsibility for deciding things, it is a demonstration of your authority.

Parents

- Parents possess the authority that is vested in their position as parents. You may have lost touch with this, but you can never actually lose it.

- Be aware that things such as threats and bribes, or shouting and shaming, are tools of power that children resent deeply. These behaviors will ultimately undermine your authority, not boost it.

- You demonstrate authority when you take responsibility. If things have been going badly, tell your son that he hasn't been himself, and be constant about guidelines you set.

Teachers

- If you trust a boy to behave as expected, and he in turn trusts you, this demonstrates your authority and assumes a joint responsibility for resolving any problems.

- If you make it clear from the start that your professional objective is every child's best interest, and you are able to convince him of this, he will not lose faith in you or in himself when you make a mistake.

42 Use reasons to explain, not persuade

I'm not sure why, but the more I explain to my son why I want something done, the more likely he is to sit tight and refuse to do it.

Boys deserve to be given reasons: It shows respect for their right to know and respect for their ability to understand. Hearing reasons teaches them how to put forward an argument and be rational. But often it goes wrong. Why? If you offer too many reasons, it changes what you say from an authoritative command to a much weaker exercise in persuasion.

First, children switch off at the first sound of a pleading voice because they've heard it before, they know what's coming and they feel manipulated. Second, we weaken our case by overstating it. Children are smart. They quickly see multiple reasons as a means to get them to agree, so they argue and refuse.

No more than two reasons are needed. All an adult needs to say is, "This is what I want you to do, this is why, now go and do it."

Parents

• Give no more than two reasons to explain why you want something done.

• Look him in the eye as you tell him, so you come across as serious.

• Then turn away, because this conveys the clear message that you expect him to comply. Hovering suggests he won't do it and will need policing.

• To avoid appearing too controlling when you want to say "no," ask *him* to tell you what your answer and reasons are likely to be.

Teachers

• If a student asks for something outside the accepted rules, ask him to state his understanding of the rules and guess what your answer is going to be. He then gets to the answer "no" without you having to say it.

• Use no more than two reasons to explain why a student has to do something.

43 Be fun, fair and flexible

My father grew up in a family with very strict rules. But for one day, once a year, the kids were in charge. They could do what they wanted and generally go wild—stay up late, watch movies, run around screaming. They let off steam and everyone had fun. It sounded great!

Many boys seem to enjoy the safety and security offered by structure, but they won't thrive if they feel restrained by the unrelenting grip of a grim disciplinarian.

Whoever is responsible for him will gain a boy's respect and full cooperation only if the rules stay in the background and his daily experience is, instead, characterized by fun, fairness and enough flexibility for him to feel he is listened to, loved and cared for as an individual.

Parents

- Set aside regular time for family fun, outings and games.

- At birthdays, holidays and other family events, hide presents or candy around the house as a treasure hunt to add to the fun. It shows you have made an effort to do something special for your children.

- All children love family rituals, whether weekly, monthly or annual. If these are fun, involving some relaxation of rules, the whole family will enjoy them even more.

- Flexibility, backed by a reason and a twinkle in your eye, won't lead to any loss of authority. Insensitive rigidity will.

Teachers

- Although curriculum planning and goals offer less room for flexibility, you can introduce fun into lessons through puzzles and games as alternative routes to learning.

- Try to see milder pranks as boys having fun and letting off steam. If you let them get to you, they'll do it again.

- Be creative: Adapt a lesson to address an issue currently in the headlines.

- Being fair means not just treating everyone equally but also being sensitive to the reasons for an individual's behavior or request.

44 Rules cut conflict

Discipline is the aspect of parenting that causes most parents the greatest heartache. It is also the thing most parents feel they get wrong. This isn't surprising because there is rarely a "right" answer: The rules have to shift as boys grow and circumstances change.

Creating family rules is difficult because you must balance different people's needs and demands, manage different and developing personalities and sometimes compromise between different cultures and values.

However, it is clear that, provided they are agreed on in advance and fully understood, family rules diminish conflict. It's conflict that does the harm, not rules. Clear expectations and established daily patterns reduce the number of challenges. When your boy sees you mean business, he'll stop pushing you.

Parents

- You don't avoid conflict in the long term by giving in. He'll only learn that the more he pushes, the more he gets.

- Boys in particular like the security that rules provide.

- Being rule-abiding at home will help him to be law-abiding later.

- Be clear, be fair, be firm and be consistent. Don't have too many rules, keep them simple and stick to them nine times out of ten.

- If you feel you're losing control, prioritize. Stay firm on the issues you care about most and drop the rest.

Teachers

- Clear rules, applied fairly and consistently throughout the school by all staff, help children know where they stand and feel secure.

- Involve the boys themselves whenever possible in agreeing on the rules so they don't feel so controlled and can take more responsibility.

- Have specific gradated consequences for clearly defined breaches of the rules.

45 Avoid wielding the tools of power

One friend of mine never stops talking about his father. It's never good. His father was a bully, sarcastic, critical, was alternately friendly and hostile, played him off against his brother, wouldn't accept any different point of view from his own. My friend has now spent years trying to figure himself out, getting his confidence back, feeling comfortable with disagreement and learning how to be tolerant.

The tools of power that adults use are hitting, hurting, damaging belongings, bribery, ridicule, threats, sarcasm, shouting, emotional withdrawal and withholding food and liberty. It may be tempting to use these sometimes, especially when you are running out of steam, but it is counterproductive. Boys will find ways to get back at you, to preserve what they see as their self-respect.

Our children deserve the best from us, not the worst.

Parents

- It is best not to force an issue when either you or your child is tired. Let it go, in case it blows up in your faces.

- Try using the "soft no": If he does not respond to your request right away, instead of raising your voice and issuing threats, repeat it more quietly, making sure you and he are looking directly at each other.

- Try trusting him to comply, giving one or two reasons, or use creative ways to get his compliance instead.

Teachers

- Responding with instant punishments in an apparently arbitrary way is an abuse of power. Be logical, fair and consistent to avoid resentment and to maintain students' cooperation.

- Avoid using sarcasm and ridicule in the classroom. These are not appropriate tools for confident, positive teaching.

- Don't react to challenges personally. Doing so leads to communication breakdown.

- People shout and throw things when their patience and skills have run out. Team-teach to refresh your skills if you lose control more than occasionally.

46 As the adult, it's your job to repair

My son and I couldn't see eye-to-eye. We went through one bad patch when we didn't speak for nine months.

When things have broken down, however much you think your son is at fault, it's your job as the adult to fix your relationship with him. You have the greater wisdom, maturity, confidence and skill to achieve this. Refusing to acknowledge or communicate with your son is no way to teach him how to repair relationships or to give him confidence in himself.

Parents

- When your son's behavior is awful, try not to take it personally. He will often misbehave to get attention or to protect himself, not to get at you, unless he feels he has good cause. You should not need to retaliate.

- Make the first move and take responsibility for the situation.

- Make the second, third and fourth moves. After a bad patch, trust is thin, so don't expect a quick turnaround. Making up should not depend on immediate reciprocation.

Teachers

- Personality clashes are a fact of life: Some students seem to rub you the wrong way, but it is your responsibility to work it out. Be open with the student, reflect on any past personal experiences that may explain your reactions and take responsibility. Suggesting a different teacher may be the only way out.

- Be aware that personal and professional stress can undermine skills and tolerance. If you are under stress, be open about your state of mind, apologize, state your needs clearly and your class will almost certainly offer cooperation and understanding.

47 Discipline without dictatorship

All boys need boundaries to help them control and manage their behavior and to fit into a family or school framework of rules. Boundaries and rules help keep boys safe. They help them fit in with and be acceptable to others. Rules show that you care about what happens to boys and rules get you involved in their world.

A framework of rules is essential for building self-esteem because it suggests that life will be structured, planned, predictable, have a rhythm and pattern, and be safe and positive. But only discipline that acknowledges and respects the needs of the child will achieve this. Discipline that is inflexible, that humiliates, in which the adult uses his or her physical, verbal and authoritative advantage inappropriately will, steadily and inevitably, chip away at a boy's self-esteem.

Parents

- Be clear and prioritize. Don't have too many rules. Keep them simple.

- Be firm but also friendly and loving. Stick to your rules, nine times out of ten, but be flexible when it really matters to your son.

- Be fair, because this is the best way to keep your son from becoming resentful.

- Be consistent. Try to respond in the same way each time and get your partner to do the same.

- Keep your love constant. Don't blow hot and cold.

- Set a good example: Behave as you expect him to behave.

Teachers

- Dictatorship no longer works in the classroom (if it ever did); military-style orders and insults are no longer acceptable.

- As with parents, be clear, be firm, be fair, be consistent, be fun and be flexible, giving reasons whenever you adapt or relax the rules.

- Plan for variety and use different teaching styles to engage all students naturally.

- High expectations, clear rules and goals, reasonably paced and engaging work, occasional humor and unfailing respect are far more effective than threats, sarcasm or ridicule.

48 Punishment without humiliation

My dad used to make me and my sisters sit naked at meals when we'd been "bad." He didn't beat us or anything, so he thought this was OK. I've hated him ever since.

There are effective and ineffective ways to show boys how to manage their behavior. Humiliating punishments don't work.

For punishment to work well as a learning device, it should relate directly to the outcome and not cause anger, bitterness or other bad feelings. In other words, it should be fair and leave a child's self-respect intact.

Any punishment that is designed to humiliate a boy will be felt as an attack on his person, not his behavior, and will be counterproductive. Punishments that humiliate cause shame, guilt, self-doubt and, ultimately, self-hate. They lead to resentment, antagonism and hostility. Boys are not tougher than girls. To protect himself, a boy will ultimately cut himself off from the relationship and become uncooperative. Every put-down brings its own repercussions.

Parents

- When you use punishments, try to be clear, fair, consistent, brief, loving and sensitive to their effects.

- Deal with only one behavior at a time. Don't pile on the complaints.

- Punish the act, not the person.

- Alternatives to spanking include withdrawal of privileges; restricted use of a favorite toy or pastime; withdrawal of allowance; use of a cooling-off place; a verbal telling-off; and sending to bed early.

Teachers

- Always give fair warning of any punishment you may give.

- If your school does not have a behavior policy, ask for one to be developed that contains clear and gradated consequences for clearly defined behavior.

- Don't up the ante if boys challenge you or feign indifference.

- Ensure the punishment fits the crime.

- Avoid taking challenges personally or your punishments become personal too.

49 Model effective conflict resolution

Constant conflict ruins relationships and tears families apart. Children are deeply scarred by conflict, particularly when it becomes physical and involves both parents. Family conflict lies behind much teenage despair that finds expression in depression and suicide.

But we can't get rid of all conflict. Different people inevitably have different and conflicting interests that have to be reconciled. Also, each of us has times when we feel exposed and vulnerable, when we are inclined to see comments and actions as challenges and take these personally and react aggressively, even when no challenge was intended. What we can do is understand better why and when this happens, and how to manage and resolve the situation so that it does not get out of hand and those involved don't walk away feeling aggrieved, resentful, angry and ready to get back at you as soon as they can.

Resolving conflict safely and satisfactorily takes emotional maturity and skill. Children have to learn these attributes from adults.

Parents

- Good communication skills lie at the heart of successful conflict management. Listen to his case and present your case, using only "I" statements, not provocative "You" statements. Discuss compromises.

- Acknowledge the feelings and challenged interests underlying the dispute.

- You don't need to win every battle. Be prepared to walk away when the issue isn't critical, and avoid disputes when either of you is tired.

- Sibling battles teach children about conflict. If safe, let older ones resolve their problems. Younger ones will need help.

Teachers

- Schools should adopt a clear policy of nonviolence.

- Younger children can have a table where they go to talk through any dispute safely.

- All school staff can be briefed on nonviolent ways to resolve conflicts.

- Personal and social education programs should contain lessons on violence prevention and effective strategies to manage and resolve conflict.

- How teachers respond to challenges from children in class sets a powerful example.

CHAPTER 6

Responding Sensitively to Setbacks

Life presents everyone, including children, with experiences that can knock them for a loop. It is part of every school and caregiver's job to prepare the boys in their care for these ups and downs. Being bullied or excluded from groups, families breaking up, friendships ending, bereavement or separations, and disappointments at school or on the sports field are common experiences. Children can't be protected from every possible hurt, however much parents may wish to and however desirable it may be—and it may not be. But how can adults help to rebuild a boy's self-confidence when all he wants to do is run away and hide?

Most of us know a child who seems to be made of rubber and wears a permanent grin. Nothing seems to get him down. Whatever the problem, he has the ability to take the knocks, keep his attention fixed on a better future and make his way steadily, knowingly and confidently toward it. Such a boy is called "resilient." He is able to live with and through adversity, getting himself back on course, ready to move on and even to use the setback to strengthen and enrich himself.

Recovery from problems is more likely when adults respond sensitively to a boy's setbacks. When they handle his confusion and dejection well, he retains enough self-respect and self-esteem to face the world again, to try again and to treat the setback as an opportunity to grow and learn.

Resilience is sometimes described as the ability to bounce back, but this misrepresents what happens. Staying power involves action, not reaction. People with staying power think, feel, perceive and understand themselves and their situation in a way that enables them to remain positive, active and able to recognize the lessons to be learned.

What gives boys staying power? Recent studies of children who recover from setbacks show that personality plays a small part. More helpful factors are a tendency to see themselves in a good light, having at least one good, close relationship with an adult and not being exposed to too much difficulty.

Boys who bounce back have a good sense of their own worth and abilities, believe they can shape what happens to them, are able to live comfortably with uncertainty, are good at solving problems, mix well with others, can maintain friendships and are generally optimistic about life. Parents and teachers can help boys by encouraging this and responding sensitively to them.

50 Give him safe time to talk

After my parents split up, I saw my dad on weekends. He only asked how I was doing in front of other people, which let him off the hook and never allowed me to open up.

When boys feel close to someone and are able to make sense of what's happened to them, they are more likely to recover from setbacks. Talking usually helps, but the time and place must be right. There's no point in raising the issue in a place where the conversation will be overheard, when either of you feel uncomfortable, or when there's insufficient time to explore and come to some conclusion, even if that means deciding you need more time to talk.

This is particularly relevant if your son is ashamed about what has happened or if he feels responsible—if he has been bullied at school or been found cheating or stealing, for example. Children sometimes feel they're to blame for things that are their parents' responsibility, such as relationship problems. Even if they don't believe they're the cause of the problem, they may still feel guilty for not having prevented it.

Parents

- Avoid being intrusive: Always ask whether he's ready to talk.

- Make sure there is enough time before you begin talking.

- Make it clear from the start that the conversation is confidential, and get his permission to pass anything on to someone else: "Do you mind if I tell Dad/Mom/your teacher what you've said?"

- If your son finds it hard to talk, try going out for a walk together. Say you are ready to talk when he is, but let him initiate.

- Be aware that boys sometimes prefer to work things out in their own heads rather than talk.

Teachers

- Peer mentorship programs are useful during grade school and middle school.

- In the early middle school years, teachers play a vital role—they should be selected for their proven abilities in dealing sensitively with students.

- Written references to personal issues or problems should be taken seriously and responded to sensitively, not ignored.

51 Fortify his heart, don't thicken his skin

Many people believe that the best way to arm their son against verbal attack and disappointment is to thicken his skin, to get him to "toughen up." They achieve this in three ways. Some make a habit of speaking harshly to their son, just to get him used to being hurt, to create an immunity to it. Others constantly tell their son, because his emotions make him vulnerable to pain, he should deny or distance himself from them. Most often, people advise boys to strike back.

A far better way to protect him is to strengthen him on the inside—his emotions and belief in himself. The other route not only does great damage to a boy's self-esteem and self-understanding, it also cuts him off from his essential self. Suits of emotional armor stop feelings from coming out as well as from going in, and therefore offer no long-term help with managing relationships.

Parents

- Build his inner strength: Trust him. See him as competent. Let him have some autonomy over his life. Respect his view of the world and tell him you love him.

- If he's in trouble, help him. Don't put him down or say, "Why did you get yourself into this mess?"

- Encourage him to follow and trust his instincts. *Encourage* means to give courage, to "enhearten."

- Give him assertive things to say to people who hurt others: "I don't know why you need to say and do these things that hurt others" or "I don't have to listen to you." Advise him to turn away. Discuss possible strategies.

Teachers

- Constantly monitor the different ways in which you talk to boys and girls.

- Ensure that you don't speak more harshly to boys than to girls, believing that they are tougher and can "take it."

- Don't fall victim to expressing stereotypical views about girls or boys.

52 Nurture his self-respect

A boy may feel more humiliated than a girl would when he has a setback—when he believes he has let either you or himself down—because most boys assume they shouldn't get things wrong or show any weakness. If and when the problem becomes public, he won't be proud of the position he finds himself in. His self-respect will be damaged—even if he is not really to blame.

Yet what he needs to pick himself up and face the world again is a double dose of self-belief and self-respect. In other words, when he's feeling down, he will have the least of what he most needs. Whatever you feel about the incident, your primary role must be to help repair the damage done and to leave him with enough self-respect to start over again. Humiliating him won't work.

Parents

- He learns to respect himself when he sees that you respect him.

- Those who are frequently blamed or shamed have trouble holding on to their self-respect. They can retain it if they are guided, sensitively, to right their wrongs without criticism or insult.

- Self-respect grows partly from being given responsibilities and carrying them out successfully.

- Boys who shirk responsibility and are allowed to ignore the consequences of their actions have a hard time holding their heads high.

Teachers

- Show respect for them, so they can respect themselves.

- Help them to see the good in themselves and in what they are able to achieve.

- Encourage independent learning so that pupils learn to trust and respect their own judgment and don't hold themselves back for fear of being condemned as failures by others.

- Encourage students to respect each other. Always listen respectfully and share successes. Ask them to talk about one of their achievements before they were ten, between ages ten and twelve, and so on, in small groups.

53 Avoid shame and guilt

Shame and guilt are natural human feelings. When people have specific duties and responsibilities, and fall short of meeting them, it is natural that they might feel some shame or guilt. So why is it so important for a boy's self-esteem to protect him from too much shame, when the cry so often is that troublesome boys seem to be shameless?

Shame and guilt create confusion and self-doubt. They are difficult and destructive emotions for all children, largely because they mean they have let themselves or someone else down. Often they don't understand why or how. Occasionally, it is appropriate for a boy to feel shame and guilt—for example, if he's old enough not only to know how he should behave but also to manage his behavior (and therefore to be held fully responsible for it). If, on the other hand, an adult stirs up shame and guilt in a boy to punish him, it's unlikely to produce the desired result. Rather than changing his ways, it is much more likely that he will reject these uncomfortable feelings and deny responsibility for the problem.

Parents

- Make it clear that he is not to blame for any marital or relationship problems you are having.

- If he has tried to sabotage a new relationship of yours, ask how he feels about it. Don't play on his guilt.

- Address the consequences of his poor behavior, not your shame or embarrassment.

- If he is being bullied, discuss what he can do to stop it. Don't tell him he's weak.

- Let your son decide how he feels about his wrongdoing. A suitable consequence is your decision.

Teachers

- Instead of rubbing a boy's nose in his mistakes, make your expectations clear.

- Something's wrong if you often make boys feel guilty.

- Sarcasm and ridicule rarely lead to greater effort, because the shame they cause undermines confidence.

- Don't punish the whole class for something only a few have done. This produces widespread resentment, not guilt in the few.

- Don't blame students for things that are your fault. Boys are usually aware of a teacher's shortcomings and are likely to react to them.

54 Offer extra closeness

When a boy experiences stress and trouble, he will need the reassurance of the adults he depends upon even more. However, if his parents are angry or disappointed, they are more likely to withdraw than to draw closer to him. Children understand themselves through their key relationships—those they have with friends, family and professionals. If these supports disappear in his time of need, your son will doubt himself even more profoundly.

Not only will he lose confidence in himself and question his identity, he will also be further confused and upset by the altered behavior of the people closest to him.

All changes are difficult for children. In times of change and trouble, try to stay close and be around more.

Parents

- Changes that may upset your son can include moving; starting at a new school; illness in the family; bereavement; you starting a new relationship or problems in your current one.

- Depending on your son's age, you can try talking to him as he takes a bath; sitting on his bed at night; sitting next to him while he watches TV; keeping him company as he walks to the bus stop; or giving him rides in the car and chatting to him as you drive.

Teachers

- Spend time with him in a quiet corner.

- Ask him to help you with tasks.

- Find time to have short personal conversations.

- Keep reminding him that he can talk things through with you, or suggest another person he might talk to (friends, parents, another teacher or mentor).

55 Help him see the lessons to be learned

Don't despair, start to repair! Parents and teachers offer effective help when they remain nonjudgmental and let a boy figure out for himself what went wrong, or what he did wrong, and what he can do to move forward again in a practical and confident way. There is always something to be learned from a setback. Rather than playing the victim and blaming someone else, your son can take the opportunity to come through the experience stronger, wiser and more competent.

Be positive. Instead of asking, "What will you avoid doing next time?" you can ask, "What might you do differently next time?"

Not all setbacks will fit this model. If a child is feeling down because he has been bullied, had a fight on the playground, or been dumped by a girlfriend, he will not necessarily have done anything wrong. But there will still be conclusions to draw and the solution should lie with him. Problems should be reflected and acted upon, not recoiled from or removed by an overprotective parent.

Parents

- Unravel and break down the problem into pieces. If something went wrong, there will be practical reasons for it.

- Don't let your son attribute setbacks to his own general incompetence. He should not see setbacks as unalterable omens of his future but as learning opportunities.

- Ask him what he thinks went wrong. Don't tell him what you think unless he asks, or tells you he's happy to listen.

- Identifying the lessons to be learned is energizing. When he can see what went wrong, he will know how to correct it and regain control.

Teachers

- Making students aware of the control they have over daily life enhances self-confidence. Ensure that schedules and homework planners are used regularly and effectively.

- We find out about ourselves by taking responsibility. The aftermath of setbacks provides opportunities for this.

- Develop the habit in students of asking questions such as "What are the lessons to be learned?" and "What have I learned?" which both foster reflection.

- If a student doesn't finish an assignment, ask for a realistic plan to make up lost ground.

56 Hear his side of the story

When children have setbacks, it is common for parents to become emotionally involved, and the danger is that they will take the situation personally and feel shamed by it. Try not to assume, before you have heard his story all the way to the end, that your son is at fault, and don't tell him off for putting you in a difficult position with, for example, the police or his school.

If he is upset about something you consider minor, try to see it from his point of view. Adults and children perceive things differently, so avoid applying your judgments unthinkingly. Saying things like, "Stop making such a fuss," "It will pass," or "I can't understand why you're bothered by that" won't help him get over something. Helping him to think through the problem will.

By listening to his side of the story, you show that you are taking him seriously and respect his point of view, are treating him fairly and don't always assume the worst where he's concerned. All of this will help him to maintain his self-esteem.

Parents

• Let him tell you about his disappointments, and don't belittle them.

• Assume the best of him, not the worst.

• In arguments between brothers and sisters, listen to everyone's story, then ask each of them in turn to suggest a possible solution.

• A child doesn't always want you to solve his problems. He may just want to vent and be listened to. Keep your opinions to yourself unless he asks for them.

Teachers

• Don't assume he's in the wrong if he has a grievance against a teacher. Suggest he go to the counselor or principal to be heard and taken seriously in a neutral space.

• Hear his side of the story. Avoid prejudice, stereotyping and hasty judgments. Just because a boy has a reputation for causing problems, it doesn't mean he is implicated in this one too.

57 Identify the danger signs and times

When Dale was fourteen, his parents split up. The separation was amicable and he seemed to cope well. But he soon became not only disorganized but also hypersensitive. For months afterward, the slightest negative comment from classmates would result in tears and, if anyone laughed, he assumed they were mocking him.

Children's resilience is obviously low when their parents or caregivers split up, when someone close to them dies and during other forms of family upheaval. But they are particularly vulnerable when they start or change schools—grade school as well as preschool and secondary schools.

Boys' confidence also drops when they pass through key developmental stages—at the age of about eight and at the onset of puberty and adolescence. At eight, they begin to think for themselves. In middle school, "macho" culture begins to take hold as male hormones kick in, boys gain more freedom by holding part-time jobs and stop trying to please. At these times, boys especially need a lot of attention.

Parents

Teachers

- Your son will need a lot of support and attention when he starts middle school and for the next two years.

- Situations that can destabilize children include
  - domestic violence
  - racial abuse
  - constant criticism/abuse
  - home/school moves
  - divorce and separation
  - bullying
  - family reformation, gaining step-families
  - bereavement
  - a parent's absence
  - family illness/disability
  - homelessness
  - being taken into care by the state

- Troubled children will often
  - be withdrawn and lonely
  - be sad, prone to tears
  - fall asleep at school
  - have low concentration/be preoccupied
  - be reluctant to work or mix with others
  - be aggressive to others
  - be frequently bullied
  - be unable to follow routines
  - be clingy, dependent
  - need constant reassurance
  - contrive helplessness
  - cheat, lie or steal
  - destroy work on completion
  - destroy others' work
  - reject teachers' help
  - turn up late/be absent
  - be the class clown
  - be reluctant to state preferences, make choices or agree on goals

58 Deal positively with peer pressure

Peer pressure, along with bullying and drugs, is a subject that frightens many parents, and it seems that parents of boys are particularly worried about these issues. Apart from not wanting the expense of providing the hippest tennis shoes, designer clothes, and the very latest in computerized home entertainment, we like to believe that our sons will be sufficiently independent to withstand the pull of the peer group, especially when that group becomes involved in illegal activities.

Children generally love to conform and hate to be different. Their earliest flirtation with independence from parents and self-expression is frequently through the safe route of fashion, and the younger they are when they choose their own clothes, music and so on, the more likely it is that these will be the routes they choose. Keep in mind: Not all peer groups cause problems.

Parents

Teachers

• Don't drive your son into the arms of antisocial friends by being negative and constantly critical. The best way to help him resist them is to nurture his self-confidence and give him inner strength.

• If he wants expensive clothes or games, help him contribute toward their cost by saving his allowance or (if old enough) his part-time earnings.

• Ask him to question whether people who won't allow him to be different are truly friends.

• Remember, boys who are open to peer pressure are impressionable. Help him feel that he is acceptable as he is.

• Be aware of the power of peer groups to divert some boys from their studies. A peer mentorship program can offer vulnerable boys a listening ear.

• Discuss the issue of peer pressure frequently in assembly, English class or health class.

• Many boys who are seduced away from learning are vulnerable because they are already failing. Identify those who might be led astray as early as possible and offer them one-on-one tutoring help to keep them on track.

59 Keep him informed of developments

One of the most important needs we all have is to be kept informed about changes and events that affect us. We get very annoyed if employers, partners, the local government or neighbors do things that affect us without letting us know in advance. Children need to be told things, too, especially if their families are going through changes.

If you are having a trial or permanent separation or going through a divorce; if someone in the family is ill and needs a lot of medication or has to go into the hospital, perhaps for an operation; or if you are looking at possible schools for him, your son will want to know how things stand. All children can panic and think the worst, or be disappointed by an unrealistic dream, if they have only sketchy information to go on.

As stated earlier, if you keep your son informed, you show respect for his right to know, his need to understand what's happening to him, and his ability to take in that information and use it sensibly.

Parents

- Keep children informed about events and changes (before, during and after they happen); feelings (yours and theirs); decisions and facts.

- Anyone who feels uncomfortable about raising issues such as going into the hospital, dying, divorce or moving can borrow a children's book from the library that explores the subject through a combination of fiction and factual information.

- Children need to make sense of their world and what is happening around them. Keeping them informed of developments is an important way to do this.

Teachers

- Ensure that children know exactly why something is happening, from the very simplest reasons, such as what the goals of a particular lesson are, to larger issues, such as why a student is being moved to a different group or who'll be teaching the class while you are away.

60 Find good support groups

When my dad died, my life fell apart. My friends at school and the soccer team were the two things that kept me going. My friends were always there for me and the team got me out of the house and made me feel normal.

Research into what helps children and young people get through difficult personal experiences shows that they do better when they are involved in a range of groups and feel part of a wider community.

Belonging to a group can help boys

- feel secure about who they are when they might otherwise question their identity and their future
- maintain continuity by preserving their normal daily and weekly routines
- receive understanding and support from people who know them and have time for them

Parents

- Help your son to attend his regular groups and clubs during troubled times.

- If he has few commitments other than school, see if there are other activities locally in which he can become involved.

- If he's having trouble at school, outside groups can help him start new relationships with a clean slate.

- This is a time when he may be drawn into undesirable groups, so keep an eye on him.

- Don't let your need for his company isolate him from his friends.

Teachers

- Encourage boys who are having a tough time to sign up for clubs and after-school activities.

- Vulnerable boys may benefit from being kept together in stable class groups to encourage security and support.

61 Minimize conflicts at home

This is a hard one, because arguments are a natural part of family life. However, time and time again, conversations with boys have revealed how hard it is for them when home is, in their eyes, characterized by conflict. We also know from these conversations that violence and conflict in the home are associated with boys who have particularly low self-esteem.

Conflict is unsettling. When boys are going through a difficult time, and already feel unsettled, parents should make an extra effort to avoid arguments, both between themselves and with the boy concerned. When parents fight, verbally or physically, boys can feel under pressure to take sides, which splits them down the middle.

How can parents know when their family conflict is greater than "normal"? Factors that make a difference include frequency of arguments; who is involved; what the disagreement is about; whether it becomes noisy or personalized; whether verbal or physical violence, abuse or bullying are involved; and whether and how the conflict is resolved.

Parents

- Discuss cutting back on arguments during difficult times.

- Encourage everyone in the family to write down their complaints instead. You can discuss these at a set time; say, once a week.

- Be aware that personal insults, shouting and abuse will damage a boy's self-esteem.

- Discussion and debate are healthy. They are not the same as conflict.

- Teaching and modeling ways to resolve conflict will be of lifelong benefit to your son.

Teachers

- Conflict at home, especially domestic violence, can affect boys' schoolwork. Take this conflict seriously.

- Discussions about why conflict happens, and how to resolve it, should be part of all personal and social education programs.

- If boys discover that others are coping with the same problems, it may help them to cope.

CHAPTER 7

Supporting His Learning and Personal Growth

A boy who feels good about himself achieves good results and tends to do well at school. Parents and other adults who support his learning and wider personal development give him a good head start and make him feel good about himself.

To be motivated to achieve anything, a boy must believe in himself. Self-esteem and a sense of self-worth lie at the heart of successful learning and growth. "I believe I can do it" is as important as "I want to do it."

Boys feel capable when they are given opportunities to test themselves and be successful; when someone lets them know they have done well; when they have been understood, trusted and respected; when they feel physically and emotionally safe; when they feel accepted for who they are; and when others love them and enjoy their company.

If boys are punished and ridiculed; told off for trying new things, asking questions or making mistakes; constantly criticized; ignored and made to feel insignificant; or if an adult's expectations are so high that pressure and failure become unavoidable features of their lives, they will close themselves off, leaving their potential untapped.

Learning and growing involve change and taking risks, the unpleasant possibility of outright failure, facing up to limitations, and the excitement of discovering new talents. When boys feel competent and good about themselves, they are likely to be optimistic about their present and future skills and abilities. Confident boys with a sense of their own identity know their potential and therefore imagine who and what they might become. They see the unknown as exciting and a challenge.

Boys who are unsure of who they are feel the opposite. Pessimistic about what they are capable of achieving, they tend to block out negative thoughts, sidestep failure and avoid change, claiming either that they know it all already or have no need to know. These are self-protection tactics. Boys use them to avoid challenge, which will move them on. Seeing learning as "uncool" is simply one additional, highly convenient and seemingly respectable way of avoiding taking responsibility for success and failure.

Too many boys lack self-confidence to such a degree that they cut themselves off from trying to succeed at anything. Many lack positive role models of successful men who can show them what they might achieve. Boys need to be shown the learning potential in every failure and to be shown that they are capable.

62 Encourage and value
a range of skills

A boy in a depressed area of Detroit wanted to study dance.
A dance project at his school had given him a new interest
and talent. When his father found out, he was furious. He
threatened to throw his son out of the house if he went
ahead, so the boy was forced to give up his dream.

Children do best when they experience a lot of success and
believe they are good at a range of different things. The
more they experience themselves as competent, the more
likely they are to try new things. They will also widen their
skills base, which will increase their ability to cope in a
range of different situations. Academic success is by no
means the only way to value a child.

Every boy will have many talents. He may be good at
football, dancing, drawing, constructing models, climbing
trees, rollerblading or bicycle tricks. He may know a lot
about insects, animals or gardening, be good at thinking
things through or getting himself organized. He may be
quick to understand how someone's feeling, or be tuned in
to his own feelings.

Parents

- Try to broaden his base of achievement. Let him try a range of activities and skills. Libraries keep details of local children's groups and activities.

- Every child will benefit from believing he is good at something. It might be fixing his bike, playing with other children, being creative with construction sets or skilled with computers, for example.

- Limit television viewing. He needs balance and variety to get the best from himself and to feel proud and successful.

- Try to involve him in the practical things you do around your home.

Teachers

- Find something that each boy is good at, tell him he's good at it and work to develop his strengths.

- If a boy has a talent that is unusual, encourage the other children to respect his skill—but first, find out what it is.

- Work hard to break down gender-stereotypical choices for activities and community service.

- Set up after-school and lunchtime clubs to introduce students to new interests.

63 Support and encourage, don't control and push

Support and encouragement give boys the energy they need to concentrate better, stick with things, achieve more and feel good about their progress. Controlling and pushing can leave boys exhausted, resentful and inclined to give up.

When we support and encourage, we share a boy's burden and give him the courage to try new things. By contrast, when we control and push, we add to his burdens, imply that he cannot be trusted to do it on his own, sap his courage and undermine his self-belief.

Controlling, pushy adults are likely to finish tasks for their son; fill his time with activities; point out mistakes immediately; be competitive; issue threats; set new goals in quick succession; hover and get involved in homework, correcting mistakes and so on.

Parents

- Show an interest in what he does. Watch him undertake various activities. Ask how things went after he makes a special effort.

- Offer help: Take him where he needs to go. Discuss problems. Answer questions.

- Listen when he tells you about his problems and successes. Share his enthusiasm about dreams and goals. Note his achievements.

- Show trust. Help him set his own goals in a time frame he can handle.

- Discover and accept your son's learning style and preferred work patterns.

Teachers

- Give him detailed information about the progress he's made and what he still needs to do.

- Help him devise a plan of action if he gets stuck, to keep him on track.

- Be enthusiastic about his improvements.

- Use stars, stickers and incentives carefully. If boys decide it's no longer cool to work for rewards, they are left with nothing to work for.

- Letters, postcards or certificates sent to students' homes instead of public announcements remove the potential for peer ridicule and allow parents to enthuse over their sons' achievements.

64 Trust that he'll manage

I sit with him every night when he does his homework, and then I check it. If it's no good, I make him do it again.

We agreed with our twin sons when they were fifteen that they should start to save if they wanted to go to college. Both worked weekends and vacations from then on. Both took honors classes and both got all A's.

These two stories represent two very different attitudes to learning. One implies no trust, the other plenty of it.

Parents

- Managing a part-time job and schoolwork is possible if handled with common sense. Try it before you ban it. It can teach great time-management skills and looks good on college applications and resumes.

- When your son starts a new school, trust that he'll cope. Saying, "I hope you will/will not . . ." suggests you fear the opposite.

- When he's trying something, let him know you believe he can do it, then walk away. Don't hover over him expecting problems.

- If he says he's ready for an exam or a test, don't push him to go through his notes once more.

Teachers

- Ask if he thinks he can handle something. If he says yes, support him in his decision.

- Occasionally present work as a challenge. More often than not, boys will strive much harder if told, "Now, I'm not sure if this is too hard." However, use this tactic only when you firmly believe a student can cope with the work.

65 Make it safe to make mistakes

Your son will need a ton of self-belief to make the most of his potential, but he won't develop it if you jump on him every time he makes a mistake. Companies will be looking to employ risk-resilient people in the future, not frightened rabbits.

Mistakes are an essential part of learning. "Everyone gets scars on the way to the stars," wrote the songwriter Fran Landesman. The motto of one technology company is, "If everything you do is a success, then you have failed"— meaning that mistakes are a sign of creativity and the ability to take risks. Mistakes are also useful. They shed light on the task at hand. They show what does and does not work, and what needs to be done differently. Mistakes tell a story, and it is a story we need to understand.

If you are afraid of making mistakes and try to deny them, you are sending your son an unhelpful message. Business today is error-tolerant, rewarding staff for handling their errors rather than punishing them. Love him for who he is, not for what he can do.

Parents

• Admit your own mistakes and say what you have learned.

• Let him notice his own errors. Say, "I can see two problems here, can you?"

• If his homework is careless, ask whether he's doing it in the best way, at the best time and place.

• If he performs poorly under pressure, make sure he isn't investing too much in results or worrying what you'll say.

• If he makes more mistakes than usual, he may not understand something, hasn't worked hard enough, isn't using the right method or is upset about something.

Teachers

• Be honest about your mistakes, state what you've learned from them and apologize for them if appropriate.

• If a boy makes more mistakes than usual, it could be due to your teaching methods, or he's distracted or anxious about avoiding errors.

• Raise class awareness of attitudes about making mistakes by encouraging discussion. Note whether boys react differently than girls.

• Often boys respond best when involved in activities that include risk-taking. Ask them to consider why they succeeded (if they did).

66 Have realistic expectations

My six-year-old son's report card was positive about every aspect of his work and social development. When I said "Good job," he turned away and choked out, "It was a stupid report. What's the point of telling me I'm good when it's so easy?"

People perform according to expectation. They tend to live up to—or down to—their reputations. Far too many children have failed for far too long simply because they were not asked to do any better. They never realized what they could do because they had never been stretched, and they believed the limits of their capability to be those implied by the easy goals set.

A goal that is set too high is as unhelpful as one set too low. Challenges must tempt your son, not threaten him and put him off. Goals that are too high can lead to failure, ruin his confidence and make him believe that succeeding is the only way to gain your approval.

Parents

- Ask him what he thinks he can handle.

- Help him to devise clear plans for meeting his goal.

- Invite him to think ahead about any problems he might meet and how he'll handle any setbacks.

- Invite him to select short-term goals, which seem more achievable, as well as a few long-term ones.

Teachers

- Make sure the goal, deadline and quality expectations are clear.

- Encourage planning and reflective skills.

- Let the boys assess whether the conditions have been met.

- Ask for a detailed study plan if you detect overconfidence—don't tell them that the goal is unrealistic.

- Ask whether they're ready for the next challenge or want some time to let what they have learned sink in.

- Be clear, practical and realistic about your own goals.

67 Read and learn together

Boys are known to lag behind girls in speech and language development, and this often has a direct effect on their interest and skill in reading. Children need to grow up in their own way and at their own pace, and there is no value in pushing a boy to read if he is not ready to do so. However, all children find learning to read easier if they are familiar with books, are interested in what they can learn from them, enjoy just looking at the pictures in them and associate books with intimacy with people they're close to.

Grandparents, parents, aunts and uncles, stepfathers, stepmothers, boyfriends and girlfriends are all people who may have a special relationship with a boy and can help him start on the track to reading and fluent literacy by sharing books with him.

Parents

• Boys are often more interested in nonfiction than in stories. They don't have to read informational books from cover to cover. Let your son choose, but be aware that for boys, reading fiction develops reflection and is enormously beneficial.

• Don't push him to read before he shows an interest in learning.

• If fathers and other male caregivers find time to read to boys regularly, books are less likely to be regarded as "sissy" or "just for girls."

• Avoid reading practice at bedtime—he'll be too tired to concentrate.

Teachers

• Choose a range of subjects for class reading to appeal to both boys and girls, and recognize the learning advantages of reading fiction.

• Develop paired or shared reading programs so that unconfident but competent readers assist weaker ones.

• Invite local male role models to class to discuss books, poetry and drama.

• Encourage a school culture that depicts reading as both a male and female activity.

• Set up reading clubs in elementary and middle schools at which boys talk about books they have recently enjoyed.

68 Show an interest, but don't be intrusive

In all my years at school, my father never once came to a parent–teacher meeting, to watch a game or see me in a play. He figured he'd done his part by earning the money to pay the bills. It killed me, and I ended up dropping out.

This boy had successful parents. His mother was interested but his father wasn't. He clearly wanted both parents to know about everything he did that was special and significant to him. It doesn't take much to show that you're interested. It takes a question or two to initiate a conversation and follow up a point, a small moment out of the day to make a connection with a boy's life and thoughts. It does take more effort to attend evening meetings, especially if it means leaving work early, but putting yourself out and being there for him will make him feel that he's important to you and that you take his school and his learning seriously.

Adults can take this too far, however. They may ask too many questions and become intrusive.

Parents

- Ask the right questions for the right reasons, directly, or leave well enough alone. Don't try to get information deviously, because he'll almost certainly guess what you're up to, then shut you out.

- Wait for him to tell you about test results. Don't ask about them right away.

- When he comes home from school, instead of asking what happened, you can tell him what you did, then say, "Is there anything you want to tell me about your day?"

- Specific questions about getting into trouble, or what he did at lunch, speak volumes about the issues on your mind.

Teachers

- For any event you want parents involved in, don't rely on student messengers. Call or mail parents directly to ensure that all parents have the opportunity to attend.

- At parent–teacher evenings and in school newsletters, constantly stress the important role that parents can play.

- Stress that, with boys, a positive role model is vital.

- Find time to take an interest in certain personal things that are important to the boys you work with most closely, but step back if any of them seem uncomfortable about it.

69 Develop perseverance: Help him to see things through

Boys have a particular problem with seeing things through. Girls are more persistent, dogged and dutiful about doing things they have been asked to do, even if they find the task boring. They seem to be able to wait longer for a reward. Boys become bored more easily, and are less inclined to put up with poor-quality teaching or coaching that does not provide variety and stimulation.

Perseverance is important. The best-laid plans can come to nothing without it. The motivation may be strong, and the goal may be clear, but if a boy doesn't have the stamina to stick with it when he comes up against an obstacle, the work he has already invested may be wasted.

Boys may give up easily because they lack confidence. If you recognize this pattern, build up their self-belief at every opportunity.

Parents

- If he gets stuck, don't belittle him or hand him the answers. Lead him to them so that he can find them himself and gain confidence to try next time—then back off.

- When he shows signs of flagging, take an interest in him and ask him to read to you, show you what he's done or tell you what he has enjoyed and what was difficult.

- If you use rewards, offer small short-term ones, not a big one a long time away in the future.

- Ensure that goals are reachable in his eyes, and that he makes a realistic plan.

Teachers

- Boys need work, and rewards, delivered in short, sharp chunks. Keep all goals in clear view, with clear routes to each one, so that their interest does not wane.

- If a student gets stuck or loses interest in a project, jointly prepare a plan for getting back into it.

- Delay work that requires deeper concentration until later in the lesson, when the boys' interest has been sharpened.

- Introduce variety into lessons and divide them into defined phases. Include hands-on activities, quizzes and regular summaries of what's been achieved in each phase.

70 Support the school

Boys, as we have seen, are growing up in a male culture that questions the value of social and academic success. No single person can change that culture. What we can do to encourage boys to believe that it's cool to succeed, however, is strengthen the ties between home and school, and support each other.

If parents respect schools and schools respect parents, there will be fewer cracks for boys to fall through, particularly during the earth-moving time of adolescence. Parents who distance themselves from their son's school and its events not only create split loyalties, but also make it easier for boys to team up with the troublemakers rather than the teachers.

Parents

• Avoid complaining about your son's school in front of him, even if you're unhappy with it.

• Whenever possible, both parents should attend meetings about a boy's progress in school. The absent parent should call his teacher for a summary.

• Try to make time to watch him take part in school events. Avoid saying, "Not another thing that school/club/you want me to do!"

• Attend fundraising events with your son so that he feels part of the school.

• Help him remember the things he's been asked to bring to school.

Teachers

• Let parents know when things are going well, not only when there may be problems, so that they can feel proud of their sons and therefore good about themselves.

• Take parents' worries seriously, and respond to their concerns with respect.

• Avoid appearing to criticize a boy's parents: "Didn't your mom know you'd need a bag lunch for today's trip?"

• At parents' evenings, focus on what parents can do to help their boys set and achieve realistic, short-term goals in learning.

71 Respect his teachers

It's much harder now than when I started teaching twenty-five years ago. It's not so much the constant changes to what we're expected to teach or the extra paperwork; it is the parents and the students who show us so little respect now. When children hear parents putting us down at home, it's hard for them to accept our authority and take work seriously when they're here.

Schools and parents need to be partners, working with each other, not against each other, if children are to do well.

Children need to trust their teacher if they are to engage completely with learning. Constant complaining about teachers at home, especially about a particular one, will encourage a boy to block out whatever that teacher is trying to teach.

Parents

- At all times, try to see the teacher's commitments and perspective, even if you take your son's side.

- Teachers are people, too. They have personal lives and sometimes go through hard times. They like to hear good news as well as bad. Most do their best and are stretched close to their limit.

- Don't be too shy to tell teachers what seems to work best for your son. They can't know everything.

- It's only fair to the teacher and your son to tell the school if there's a problem at home that might affect his behavior or work in school.

Teachers

- These days, we all have to earn the respect we feel is our due. Don't put parents down. Try to see things from their point of view.

- Be aware that vulnerable parents are likely to take your treatment of their son personally, as if you're doing it to them. Respecting every boy in your care contributes to a respectful home–school relationship.

- Send home good news, not just bad.

- At parent–teacher evenings, take parents' concerns seriously, and end with, "Is there anything else?" You can arrange an alternative time to meet if the issue demands it.

72 Channel competition creatively

Almost all boys have a competitive urge. Channeled reasonably, sensitively and creatively, it can help develop their motivation, their capacity to achieve and their sense of self. Exploited carelessly, it can lead to anxiety, despair and a decision to give up.

Boys will do best when they are encouraged to compete against themselves, when they focus on doing better than *their* last best effort. This way, their self-confidence can remain intact. The danger comes when they try to perform to impress friends or adults, set their sights on beating others and invest their self-worth in the result. Even though a boy may have tried really hard and prepared well, others might have tried harder, or simply have a more natural talent. Whenever the outcome is not completely in his control, there is the chance that he'll fail because of anxiety, and his self-esteem may suffer.

Parents

• It is better to identify a specific goal—"Try to improve the grade on your chemistry lab work"—than a general one—"Go for an A this time."

• Don't fuel competition between brothers and sisters. Each child needs to be successful in his or her own way, and accepted unconditionally for who he or she is.

• Avoid competing against your son, especially if your intention is to spur him to greater effort. It doesn't work.

• Fun competitions are fine: "See if you can beat me to the top of the stairs" is a great way to get him to go to bed.

Teachers

• Research shows that teaching based on competition produces anxious children.

• Encourage children to perform to improve, not impress, and give them feedback so that they can see the progress they've made.

• Try playing musical chairs in two ways: First, as usual—removing chairs and children each round—and second, telling the children to find other laps to sit in as chairs disappear. Ask which version they prefer. Cooperative games show how much fun it can be just to join in.

73 Failure lights the path to success

All boys experience failure—lots of it. A boy will almost certainly fail when he first tries to walk; he won't master buttons on his first attempt, ride a bike or tie his shoelaces right away, yet he is prepared to try again. Why is it that these early failures don't make growing boys give up, despite sometimes intense frustration, while later ones can stop them in their tracks and throw them into the depths of misery?

The uncomfortable truth is that adults are often responsible for the change. They start reprimanding children for failing, teasing them and making them feel ashamed.

But failure is not something to be shunned. It provides factual and neutral information on what went wrong and what needs to go right. Failure is an inevitable and essential part of learning, and shows that learning is happening at the frontier of a person's current knowledge. If the lessons to be learned from failure are taken on board, they will light the path to success. This will not happen if adults deny, ignore or punish failures, making a boy feel he should hide and ignore the truth.

Parents

- Respond constructively: Failure is like a puzzle to be solved, not a disaster to be denied. Consider whether the goal was too ambitious.

- Respond sincerely. Be honest about the outcome, and make sure it remains his problem, not yours.

- Respond sensitively. However much he may deny it, failure is upsetting and can undermine confidence. Accept, understand and let him voice his feelings. Don't be too strict with him. Seek success elsewhere to balance a failure.

- Show that you love him for who he is, not what he can do.

- Don't punish him for failing—he may start to lie or cheat.

Teachers

- Describe in detail what went wrong and how to do better.

- Let him know you believe he can improve and demonstrate this with a sample piece of work.

- Encourage him to self-evaluate as much and as accurately as possible.

- Be available if he needs help.

- Look for modest, not unreal, success stories: Individual boys can explain how, and perhaps why, they turned themselves around.

- Find out what might lie behind an unexpected drop in performance.

74 Watch him doing something he enjoys

I lived for soccer. I played a lot and got really good, being goalie for a man's team when I was fourteen. My dad lived too far away to watch me, but my mom didn't come either. Guarding the goal's a big responsibility. It got to be too much. I couldn't tell the team how I felt. After two years, I quit. I was too stressed.

Anything that is important to us, we want to share. Children are the same. Children usually enjoy doing the things they do well, so one reason to watch them is to let them show off a little and accept the pride they feel in their achievement. Watching involves you further in your son's life. It increases togetherness even when he's doing something on his own. Your presence alone will boost his self-esteem.

If your son loves playing football, riding bikes or conquering playground equipment, watching certainly takes effort and may involve getting muddy, cold or wet. You may be mystified by his passion for strange war-based, card or computer games. But he will thrive in the warmth of your watchful eye.

Parents

- Find the time to watch.

- "Mom, can I show you how I . . . ?" or "Dad, come and see me do . . ." should be answered with "Sure," but preferably not with "later" added.

- Let him impress you. Tell him afterward how much you enjoyed watching him.

- Within his hearing, tell his grandparents how well he's doing, so that he can feel pride in his skills. If they are no longer with you, you can say: "Grandma would have loved to have seen you do that."

Teachers

- You can't watch what the boys and girls in your class do in their personal time, but you can find a moment to hear about something they have done.

- Try to value whatever it is a boy enjoys doing or achieving.

- Provided that your family and work commitments allow for this, it can be gratifying for students to see their teachers attending plays, football games, concerts and so on.

75 Don't invest your self-worth in his success

Every time I did well at something, my mom would rush off and tell the whole neighborhood. She treated it as her achievement, and I ended up feeling used, empty and angry.

Although parents and teachers are naturally pleased when their sons and students do well, it is dangerous when adults begin to rely on a child's success for their own sense of self-worth.

It can damage a boy's self-esteem in a number of subtle ways. If parents feel good about themselves only when their child succeeds, they are, in effect, stealing success from him. This will leave him feeling used, confused and empty instead of fulfilled. Only additional, and repeated, success will restore his sense of achievement, which often leads to the burden of perfectionism. He will also come to believe that he is valued solely for what he can do, not for who he is.

Parents

- If you want to tell other people about your son's achievements, ask his permission. Then think about whom you want to tell, and why.

- Avoid setting a new goal for your son as soon as he has reached one. Do you benefit in some way from the pressure you're putting on him?

- Ask yourself whether you have higher expectations for your sons than for your daughters. Do you identify more closely with your son for some reason?

- Remind yourself it's his success, from his effort, and that it's his to hold on to.

Teachers

- Good teachers deliver more than results. To keep yourself from becoming too hooked on results at times when you're at the risk of doing so, list some other things you are eager for your students to develop and achieve.

- If you think you may become success-dependent, list all the other things you are good at that give you pleasure.

- If one group's results are not good, and you are becoming depressed as a result, put yourself back in control. List the things you could do differently next time that might change the outcome.

76 Let him be responsible for his success and failure

The moment of victory is far too short to live for that alone.

—Martina Navratilova

Success and failure tend to be overlaid with moral significance: It is considered good to succeed and shameful to fail. Parents can become infected by this way of thinking so that, if their son succeeds, it is their success and, if he fails, it is their failure. This can be damaging as well as confusing.

When parents "own" their son's success, they effectively steal it from him and it may lead him to fail in the future. They may do it to make themselves feel good, and run to tell others the good news, or they may take credit for his success, implying that he couldn't have done it without them. Either way, if success is always taken away, a boy may eventually turn on his tormentors and refuse to play, or burn out through his own perfectionism.

Taking responsibility for his failure is equally unhelpful. A parent's shame may lead to punishment or trivialization. Because the son does not take responsibility for his mistakes, he will be unable to progress.

Parents

- Have realistic expectations and accept him unconditionally.

- See success as neutral feedback. It shows what he's doing right. Glory shouldn't come into it.

- Help him feel comfortable with his feelings of delight or disappointment, frustration or sadness.

- If his failures become your personal shame, you hinder his chances to learn lessons.

- A failure is a sign that he's at the frontiers of his knowledge, taking risks. Discuss why it happened and what he can do differently next time.

- Your son's success is his. Don't steal his thunder by taking credit for his success.

Teachers

- Always congratulate a student on his success, and give him credit for it.

- Describe in detail what he did right and the things that led to his success, so that he knows how to repeat it next time.

- Offer some unpressured time at his new level, with time to adjust to and accept his success. Then enable him to move forward.

- Take the shame out of failure. Failure merely tells him what he needs to do differently. Personal insults will encourage him to hide behind excuses.

CHAPTER 8

Encouraging Confidence and Independence

Management trainers say the world is made up of three types of people: Those who make things happen; those who watch things happening; and those who notice nothing until afterward, and then ask, "What happened?" Children who develop sound confidence are more likely to fall into the first category when they become adults. If you make things happen, you control your own life. The ability to manage independence creatively and safely gives us tremendous advantages.

But confidence, of course, ebbs and flows. We may feel confident in some situations and terrified in others, relaxed with some people and uncertain with others. This largely depends on what we feel we're good at and how well we know the people we're with. Apart from these fluctuations, confidence also dips naturally at certain stages of child development, which happen at different times for boys and girls.

Studies show that boys' self-esteem is a picture of extremes, with more boys than girls in the highest and lowest self-esteem groups. Girls show a stronger thread of confidence running through both the medium-confident and exceptionally confident groups, but there are more confident boys than girls as a whole (25 percent compared to 21 percent). Boys in the middle group are more insecure than girls in the middle group and there are also more boys than girls at the lower end (12 percent compared to 8 percent). Boys are most confident at fourteen (when confidence plummets for most girls) and least confident at nineteen.

Today mixed messages go to children so that when they are small, they often get responsibility and power before they are ready for it, at a time when parents should remain in command. However, during adolescence, just when they need to feel confident and take control into their own hands, we tell them that it is a frightening world out there and, in effect, that they cannot be trusted to cope by themselves.

If, while he is a boy, you show trust and confidence in him, and have provided an emotionally safe, predictable environment for him, he won't become isolated during adolescence when uncertainty and self-doubt can make socializing painful. While most of us have times when we want to be alone or handle things by ourselves, spending too much time avoiding people and problems can distort boys' sense of reality and ultimately dent their courage.

77 Offer him safety, security and predictability

The Concise Oxford Dictionary defines "confidence" as "firm trust; assured expectation; boldness."

Nobody can develop self-confidence if he neither trusts himself nor has the assured expectation that other people's behavior is trustworthy and predictable. Boys who do not have a measure of consistency and predictability in their lives will find it very hard to acquire the necessary trust—in others or in themselves—to become either truly self-confident or genuinely independent. When adults behave in an arbitrary and neglectful way, they undermine a child's confidence and generate emotional dependency.

Routines help to nurture both trust and security. If a boy's key caregivers clearly trust him and provide consistency, he can begin to trust himself, his judgment and the behavior of other people. Parents don't make their son independent by disappearing from his life and letting him fend for himself; they do it by being there for him.

Parents

- Ask yourself whether your son will begin each day with a clear idea of what's going to happen and when, in terms of routines, events, or people with whom he will be involved.

- Try to ensure that he sees any absent parent regularly.

- Make your own behavior toward him as reliable and predictable as possible. If you have mood swings, or your routine has to change, try to explain why.

- Consider whether there's anything you can do to increase a sense of order and "assured expectation" in his life.

Teachers

- Boys benefit when lessons have a clear structure and purpose, and the aims and objectives are made clear at the start, so they know what to expect.

- Boys work best when given tightly structured tasks that channel their speaking and listening energies and skills in purposeful directions.

- Let them know well in advance if there are to be any changes to the normal school day or lesson.

78 Nurture his social skills

Boys, typically, tend to have less well-developed language, social and communication skills than girls. They are born more restless than girls, and are likely to have more trouble controlling their thoughts and behavior, preferring to express themselves through action rather than words. They find it harder to understand or explain the reasons for their own or other people's behavior. They need to develop these reflection skills to learn tolerance, compatibility and emotional literacy.

Increasingly, employers look for good social skills in job applicants. They want people who are happy to forge a range of relationships, who can work together in teams, who can discuss and sell their ideas and develop the empathy and understanding to handle disagreements. The ability to behave in this way lies at the heart of successful and comfortable working and socializing.

Socially adept boys who make and maintain close relationships are less likely to get into trouble when challenged. Boys need help to express themselves honestly and safely—through words rather than physical aggression or withdrawal.

Parents

- Involve him in your social life whenever appropriate to show you like being with him and trust him to behave well.

- Try to be sociable yourself. If he sees you mixing confidently with others, he'll learn from you.

- Encourage friendships: Invite his friends over, see if there's a social or sports group he can attend regularly, limit solitary activities such as computer games.

- Reading will develop his ability to reflect and empathize. Talk to him as much as you can. Ask for his views, tell him what you've done and really listen when he talks to you.

Teachers

- Include paired and small-group work in your classes so that boys learn to listen, talk, respect and compromise.

- In mixed classes, ensure that boys work with girls to pick up alternative ways of thinking, doing and learning.

- Seating arrangements are important. It can matter a lot to boys whom they sit next to.

- Encourage discussion, listening and reflection. When boys develop these skills, and think before they write, the standard of their work rises.

- Invite local sports or pop stars to come and discuss favorite books, poetry and drama.

79 Offer him opportunities to test himself

Confidence flows from competence. When a boy feels he can do things well, when his experience of himself is of one of success and overcoming obstacles rather than failing and falling short, his confidence will grow by leaps and bounds.

The more skills he acquires the better, but he won't achieve anything if he just watches TV all the time or is constantly told that he's useless. Get him out and about as well, to ensure a good balance in his leisure activities. Avoid gender stereotyping when you suggest new things he could try.

When the time is right, letting him have a taste of the world of work will help to increase his confidence about his possible future and let him see you functioning in a different role outside the home. He may wish to work part time or, if it's relevant or feasible, he could occasionally go with you to work. Schools increasingly organize work experience for their students, but extra tastes before and after such placements will add to the benefits.

Parents

- Every journey begins with a first step. He won't be as good as you, but he'll need to feel competent from the beginning. Teasing him for incompetence will set him back.

- Vacation activities (such as camp) and afterschool clubs can introduce boys to a range of new skills.

- Involve him in the jobs you do—cooking, cleaning, car washing, weeding, do-it-yourself projects, balancing the checkbook or caring for others—and be tolerant of the extra time it may take.

- Let him try out his thoughts and opinions on you and respect them. Don't compete.

Teachers

- Boys need to be encouraged to volunteer for tasks. Create special tasks, tailored to them, as an added incentive.

- Encourage any boy who seems to lack friends, confidence and social skills to socialize in a variety of ways.

- Drama can be used effectively in many lessons to enable boys to try out new roles and learn new skills.

80 Work to and from his strengths

Any boy will learn more easily, perform better and be more self-motivated if he can do things in a way that suits him (using his best senses, such as sight, sound or touch) and through subjects that interest him. A child's all-important sense of mastery—how effective and competent he feels—will develop best when he is allowed to start from who, and where, he is.

Success breeds success. All educators know that when a child is good at one thing, his new confidence will help him to do better elsewhere.

Starting from the strengths your son has not only validates him but also demonstrates the vital unconditional acceptance that gives a boy the freedom to learn and develop in his own way. The more you ignore his preferences and impose your own, the more likely he is to lose touch with himself.

Parents

- Identify his skills and strengths. Concentrate on what he can do, not on what he can't.

- Don't belittle any talent that he values.

- Think about his preferred ways of working and learning, and his particular passions. Don't force him to work in ways that go against his natural inclination.

- If poor concentration stops him from reading fiction, you could read the first few chapters to help him get into a book; try a series (the characters and story lines will soon become familiar); or read short stories—science fiction, for example.

Teachers

- Boys like being adventurous, taking risks and performing to show off their verbal wit. Drama uses these talents and can be a path to enjoying English class.

- Discover a student's passion, apply it to your subject and let him fly. Boys concentrate better when they're interested.

- Quizzes are favorites among boys: They challenge and feed their competitive instinct.

- Young boys' play often seems more vigorous and less verbal and fluent than girls'. Build on it; don't stop it. Encourage the development of story lines and characters using toys, models and, sometimes, girls.

81 Independence without abandonment

Independence should be given to children when they are ready, not because it is convenient for an adult, and regardless of whether it is appropriate to the boy's age, maturity and wishes. Sometimes, a family's practical needs are the catalyst for granting further independence, and it comes at the right time. However, it is important to judge whether your son's extra freedom is simply a convenience for you, and to be aware how he may view your motives. Do not give him too much too soon, exploit him or leave him feeling abandoned. Although he may appear able to cope, in reality he may still feel he needs your company, guidance and attention but be too proud to say so.

If a boy feels put upon, used, exploited and abandoned, or uncomfortable with the extra responsibility that goes with greater freedom, his self-reliance and self-esteem may be damaged, not enhanced. He may feel anxious and out of his depth, which will increase any lingering self-doubt and destroy his confidence.

Parents

- The first few times he does something new, stay close by or within easy reach, so that he knows he's not entirely on his own.

- Apply the idea of "supported independence" to check whether he feels abandoned. Friends may be able to provide this support.

- Ask him if he's truly happy with the arrangements you have made for him to travel, cope with a situation or be by himself.

Teachers

- Independent learning is important, but students will continue to need support.

- Boys need help with time management. For projects with a deadline, schedule times when you will be available for consultation well before the delivery date.

- Suggest that students divide their work into "bite-size" chunks. Set deadlines for sections to help steer them and to prevent anyone from falling behind.

- Tasks and responsibilities should carry clear guidelines.

- Ask what help a boy thinks he may need on solitary projects.

82 Monitor and supervise— from a distance

One night I was due home by eleven. My friends and I cooked up other plans, so I called home with some made-up story about why I needed to stay the night with one of them. Mom just did not buy it and stuck to her guns. Afterward, I was glad. I realized I wasn't sure what might have happened that night.

All the research shows that boys who get into trouble stay out for long periods of time without having to report their comings and goings to anyone at home. Monitoring and supervision help to keep boys on track when they are exploiting their newfound freedom, but it should be done sensitively and from a distance so that they don't feel insulted by any perceived lack of trust.

Being aware of your son's movements is vital. It helps to keep him safe because he knows you're aware and that you care. If you leave him to his own devices, he may flounder, feel neglected and then get back at you by actively looking for trouble.

Parents

- Each time he goes out, discuss and agree on times for calling and coming home. When he comes in, casually ask him what happened and how things went.

- If you are worried, check his story with his friends' parents. Make sure you have their phone numbers.

- Follow up if he's late getting home, so he knows you've noticed and you care. Try to be awake on his return so you can judge what condition he's in.

- Check the atmosphere of the place where he hangs out and get to know his friends.

- Keep a regular eye on his bedroom. It will give clues to work or personal problems. This is not license to go through his personal belongings, however.

Teachers

- Be alert to any pattern in missed deadlines. Consult with colleagues if you are worried.

- Closely patrolling children won't help them learn to manage and monitor themselves. Keep an eye open at break times, but from an appropriate distance.

- Records of grades for class and homework, lateness, and major incidents of bad behavior are easy to keep. Keep track of other less obvious signs of personal trouble, too, such as tears, visits to the school nurse and changes in personal appearance.

83 Develop responsibility and safe risk-taking

Research shows that, from birth onward, boys are more inclined toward risk-taking than girls. They are less reflective about any implications and therefore less thoughtful and cautious. Encourage safer risk-taking by letting your son know you care, by improving his thinking and reflective skills and, most crucial, by ensuring that his responsibilities grow in line with his rights. Responsibility is important. Through it, we find out what we can do, we feel trusted, trustworthy and respected, and we gain in competence, which in itself contributes to safer risk-taking.

A boy should grow up with appropriate and increasing experience of responsibility, beginning with things such as cleaning up after himself, getting his school things ready and taking care of sports uniforms and equipment. Later, he can take reasonable and progressive responsibility for other things, which also encourages task commitment. Nevertheless, the ability to take risks is important. Be tolerant of the mistakes your son will inevitably make while he's learning to take responsibility.

Parents

- When your son asks for more independence, try to give it to him. If the particular freedom he seeks causes problems, discuss an alternative change that will satisfy him. He'll then have less need to struggle and prove himself.

- Be aware of his coordination skills and physical strength, and keep his risk-taking in line with his physical abilities.

- Rights matched by responsibilities can encourage safer behavior, but all boys, especially adolescents, will take risks at some point. Talk to your son about safe risk-taking and trust, and set clear limits to his freedoms.

Teachers

- Learning involves taking responsibility and risks. When kept in balance, these offer useful lessons for life.

- Challenging boys, or those with low self-esteem, may respond well to being given special tasks and responsibilities.

- Boys who undertake death-defying acts may be mirroring the irresponsibility they perceive in adults close to them. Be attuned to the reasons behind high-risk behavior.

- Address the pros and cons of risk-taking in physical education lessons and assemblies. Explore the need for thrill and excitement and the psychological role it plays.

84 Encourage self-management

When the parents of our new freshmen first come in to school, they get the speech about how to beat the macho boy culture that so often takes hold. We discuss how they can help to resist it, and one of the first things I say is, "Stop doing everything for him—get him to cope with and handle life on his own."

It can be hard to let go. With such busy lives, we may feel we have fewer ways to demonstrate our love and commitment. One remaining way, as our sons grow up and become harder to hug, is to tend to their needs. Teachers say that boys start secondary school noticeably less independent and competent than girls, which affects their ability to study. We may unconsciously feel uncomfortable teaching boys to use the washing machine, cook or iron. Boys can be so clumsy, too. We'd rather do the job for him than see him struggle, ruin it or go out looking scruffy or without something because he's forgotten to think ahead.

But it is not helpful to spoil boys. It keeps them dependent and prevents them from developing the skills they need for managing school, work and their time.

Parents

Teachers

- Encourage financial independence. Give him a regular allowance and stick to the agreed amount.

- Encourage planning skills. If you're planning a family event, ask him to find out opening times and costs as a fun project for him. Give him a budget and sole charge of the family money for the day.

- You can start early by leaving him to put on his shoes, wash his own face, get his things ready for school and so on.

- Be sure that you are doing enough for him in other ways so that he knows you still care.

- Make sure you inform parents of the educational payoffs of self-reliance— that children who can take care of themselves are also successful learners.

- Don't be tempted to let boys off the hook because they are inclined to be less organized.

- Boys who live between two sets of parents may have trouble remembering to bring in their books, especially at first. It's better to give a boy two sets than to scold him and add to his problems.

- Promote the use of calendars and homework planners.

- Address time-management, work and planning skills.

85 Let him say no

Self-esteem gives boys the power to say an emphatic "No!"—
to their friends or to an adult who is behaving in a
frightening or strange way. Boys who are expected to be
"good" all the time, and who need to please someone in
order to feel accepted, will find it much harder to withdraw
from potential danger when this may involve being teased,
rebuked or cold-shouldered.

Sound self-confidence is one route to staying safe, and
parents and other caregivers will therefore need to nurture
self-esteem as the core of confidence. But boys will also need
some practice. They can't turn from habitual "yes" boys into
fierce "no" boys in one try. Many parents may feel, not
without reason, that their sons are already too smart-alecky
and need no further encouragement. But insolence isn't
exactly what is required. The right preparation includes
being given the freedom to disagree; being able to to stand
up for themselves with reasoned arguments, not fists; and
learning to respect their own judgment.

Parents

• Avoid rebuking your son for having views that differ from your own. He should feel confident about being in a minority of one if necessary.

• Allow him to express his feelings. If it's OK to feel angry, sad or excited at home, it will be easier for him to respond honestly and decisively in potentially dangerous situations.

• Let him know that you trust his judgment.

• Listen to him well when he wants to tell you something.

• Respect his choice of friends. Criticize them too often and he's more likely to ignore your reservations about serious issues.

Teachers

• Our economy, and therefore our educational focus, are changing radically. Employers no longer need or want armies of robots or lemmings. Ritual obedience is out of date, although respect certainly isn't. Older children, especially, must be given the space to disagree within boundaries of mutual respect.

• Listen. Respect a boy's right to see things differently and say so, provided he is polite. Listening doesn't mean that you have given in to him.

• Explore the room for compromise. He may have a good case, which can be responded to in another way.

86 Teach coping and survival skills

The best way to learn to handle some problems is through experience. Experience lessens fear and also helps to build common sense. Hiding from fears makes them grow. Staying indoors or in a car does not build life or street skills, and protecting boys, or girls, from the world is not responsible parenting. Getting out and about together, walking, cycling and taking public transportion teach a certain geographical sense and street awareness. Going out for night walks will help your son to respect, but not not fear, the dark.

Staying indoors most of the time does not encourage physical fitness, either. The two best defenses against bullying and other dangers are strong bodies and inner confidence. When boys are fit and able to rely on their natural physical strength, it helps them not only to run away or wriggle free but also to feel confident and come across to others as someone they don't want to mess with.

Discuss different ways of coping with such situations with your son, including how to reduce risk and protect himself.

Parents

Teachers

• Useful risk-reducing strategies include staying in public view and populated places; avoiding back stairs and alleys; going out in a group (preferably with people you know and trust); carrying money safely—a small amount in a wallet or pocket and the rest elsewhere.

• Practice verbal responses too. A sharp word delivered quickly is safer than a punch.

• Ask if he's worried about anything, and discuss it.

• It's important that he feels confident. Don't dent his confidence by predicting disaster.

• If it is practical, organize a regular walk-to-school day or week.

• Include safety and survival issues in physical education classes, but keep all discussions as positive as possible. Fear of "stranger danger" can get out of hand and undermine children's confidence.

87 Enter the forbidden zones

Sex, alcohol and, increasingly, drugs in every form are inevitable features of growing up for our sons. Do not allow these topics to become off-limits areas in your family. Although boys need their private space as they enter their teens and will defend this (sometimes aggressively) against parental intrusion, and, although it's hard to hit the right note and avoid sounding uncomfortable, it is important to keep talking. You must maintain communication in case serious problems arise.

Boys have a tendency to boast, exaggerate and fabricate to gain status and attention. When friends begin to boast, a boy will feel under pressure to claim that he, too, has "been there and done that." The reality is that he will almost certainly experiment. By the age of fourteen, one in three boys will have tried drugs. Telling a boy not to do something when peer pressure is strong may not have much impact, but suggesting that he remain in control of and true to himself by doing things only when he feels it's right may give him that ounce of extra courage to say "No" and stand up for himself.

Parents

- At home, talk openly and comfortably about sex in general conversation, so the subject is not alien.

- If talking about sex, alcohol and drugs is difficult, give your son something to read. Many leaflets and books are available about safe sex, drinking and drug use. Your school or healthcare provider will help.

- Be quietly vigilant: Inform yourself and watch out for signs of drug or alcohol use.

- If you begin a new relationship during your son's puberty, be aware that he will find the sexual side of it very difficult. Be discreet; don't compete.

Teachers

- Most primary and secondary schools have sex and drug education programs. A staff member with the right professional and personal skills and knowledge should give this program a high profile.

- High self-esteem and good social and communication skills are the best defenses against premature sexual activity, early pregnancy and drug use. All teaching should reflect this.

- Physical education and health teachers should possess excellent group-work skills to enable all students to participate comfortably and confidently in sex and drug education. They should also treat the subject seriously.

88 Promote self-direction

People don't resist change, they resist being changed.
                                        —Gerard Nierenberg

One form of independence is self-direction. Children who are self-directed are able to manage tasks and problems independently. They experience autonomy—a degree of control over themselves, being able to influence at least some aspects of their life that are currently important to them. Boys who are given no chance to direct themselves, or who lack the skills or confidence to do so, feel helpless and depend entirely on others to move forward.

Self-direction and independence feed each other. The more self-directed boys are, the better they can handle independence. The more appropriate independence they have, the more they develop the confidence and skills to become self-directed and self-reliant, and to show initiative and creativity.

A boy's first experience of self-direction will be responding to his own basic needs for food, warmth, comfort and attention.

Parents

- Directive parents create dependency: The more you tell boys what to do, the less competent they feel and the more they need you.

- Give an allowance as soon as he can handle it. Then he can spend without reference to you.

- When children feel helpless, they soon feel hopeless.

- If you feel he should change something, involve him in deciding when and how. If he wants to change something, cooperate.

- To become self-directed, boys need free time. Filling his every moment doesn't help him.

Teachers

- Students improve when they have a clear understanding of what to do to make progress. Be specific about objectives and goals.

- Asking a boy, "Do you want to do this task this way or that way?" helps him to feel he has some control over what he has been asked to do.

- Once he has a target, ask him how he plans to reach it.

- Encourage him to think, plan ahead and manage his own time to meet his needs and yours.

- Encourage self-appraisal as part of the process.

CHAPTER 9

Checking Out Your Role and Feelings

This is where we come back to basics. Despite a growing emphasis on the power of genes and the acknowledged pull of the peer group, parents and other key adults are in a strong position to influence how boys turn out and affect the faith a boy has in himself, how competent he feels and thus his overall self-esteem. A child can be born with a predisposition to be positive about life and himself, or negative about it. Close adults can either build him up or undermine him. Many families contain two male offspring who couldn't be more different from each other. Some boys need a lot more support than others. It is our role as adults to provide, as much as possible, the conditions within which a boy can feel secure and capable, not uncertain and incapable. He must feel able to influence his life, not merely to react to events and be a victim. He needs values, direction and the capacity to devote himself to and enjoy activities, causes and people, not to be rootless, isolated or completely self-centered.

We can influence but cannot always be in control or even manage our own behavior as we would wish. Outside factors intervene, and stress, uncertainty and change impair our ability to be as effective as we need to be. Frequently, a boy's behavior will test us to our limits. He contributes to the relationship dynamic, too, and as he approaches adulthood, he is increasingly accountable for his own behavior. If we have provided most of the basics, accepted his imperfections as well as our own and demonstrated our overall commitment in a way that satisfies him, we are giving him a firm foundation on which he can build.

Our feelings, hopes and fears about ourselves and our children inevitably color what we say and do. No human being is saintly enough to put others' interests constantly before their own. Children demand, and need, a great deal of time and attention. Giving as much as they sometimes want drains your reserves. You may wonder whether anything of yourself remains. If you do not consciously take time to regularly recharge your batteries (to maintain and develop your own self-esteem), you may find yourself putting up protective barriers in a desperate, arbitrary way— holding onto yourself, but also cutting yourself off from your child when he needs you most.

The best way to help your children grow up happy and healthy is to make sure that you also continue to grow and enjoy your life, both within your family and outside it.

89 Cherish and trust yourself

While you are taking care of him, you must also take care of yourself. We don't need to be told that the better we feel about ourselves, the better we cope with challenge and problems and the nicer we are toward those we live and work with. We all know this. We know, too, that when we have had a bad day or are very tired, we tend to take our frustrations out on our nearest and dearest. Taking care of ourselves is an investment that benefits others, because when we behave well, we feel positive toward other people and pass on our feelings to them.

It can be hard to trust your competence during every stage that children pass through and with every issue that presents itself. Most parents and caregivers enjoy certain developmental stages more than others. While teachers can choose whether to teach little ones or older children, parents have no choice: They have to cope throughout. Your uncertainty will be real, but children value firmness. Discuss any problems with partners and friends, carefully review your initial reactions and, if you still feel the same, trust yourself and remain consistent.

Parents

- Talk to others; it usually helps.

- Identify your little luxury, the thing that calms you down and restores your faith in yourself. It may be reading a trashy book, going to the movies or having a drink with friends.

- Make sure your choice of a pick-me-up is realistic. When grandiose schemes fail, it can have the opposite effect by bringing you down.

- Try to arrange for your personal time on a regular basis. While some things fit into small time slots, others need more time and require planning.

- "I've always wanted to . . ." —so do it!

Teachers

- Trust and believe in yourself. If you doubt your skills, you may interpret difficult behavior as a personal attack, and react defensively, provocatively and unconstructively.

- List what you see as your professional strengths, then identify where there's room for improvement. Discuss with colleagues how to share collective skills to aid professional development.

- Challenging boys make heavy demands on others. Rather than pretend to have total competence and suffer, set up a group with colleagues to pool support and ideas.

- After a bad patch, pamper, don't punish, yourself.

90 Let him be different

My father thought I had to be just like him in every way. I had to like and be interested in the same things—he even thought I should be happy to wear his hand-me-down clothes and listen to his music. Every time I tried to step away, I got the cold shoulder and he got offended. The message was clear: I was only acceptable when I followed his example.

We spend the early years of our child's life treating him as a mirror—looking for ourselves in him. It starts with his face: "He's got my eyes, his dad's nose." It then moves to his likes and dislikes: "He loves kicking balls, just like I did." All the similarities are proof that our son is part of and belongs to us—and sharing is fun. So it can come as a shock later on when we are forced to accept that he is different and may even go out of his way to be so in order to assert his individuality.

If we use our child to validate ourselves, we shackle and stifle him. Growing up is hard enough, but it will be much harder for him if we deny him the right to be different.

Parents

Teachers

• Give him room to be himself. It's your problem, not his, if you feel uncomfortable about him being different.

• Don't compete with, criticize or ridicule him. Every challenge drags him into your territory and reinforces his view that you think your methods, talents and preferences are better.

• Getting involved in his school is great, but keep it in check. All boys need space to be themselves, free from their parent's watchful eye.

• Show an interest in his choice of music, magazines, games or clothes to validate his choices, even if the current enthusiasms are temporary.

• Encourage children to be aware of themselves and their differences.

• Encourage all children to be tolerant of differences, whether they be different opinions, talents, physical characteristics or races.

• Vary your teaching methods. The way you feel most comfortable getting information across may not suit the learning styles of all the boys in your class.

91 Examine your expectations

Every family has its own history, or story. This influences what we expect for ourselves and those we live with, whether or not we want it to. There is usually a hidden agenda, which children eventually detect and react to.

These days, while we accept that education and careers are important for girls, boys still tend to carry a heavier burden of career expectation: "You'll probably be a lawyer like me," or "You should do what I did. It's worked for me." At the other end of the spectrum, if men in a family have a history of being unreliable caregivers or breadwinners, there may be low expectations for the latest generation of males.

Some typical "stories" that may influence expectations include

- "Do as I say, not as I did" (You threw away the opportunities you had, and you don't want your son to do the same.)
- "Symbol of success" (You are a success in your field, and his success will be another feather in your cap.)
- "Missed opportunities" (You want your son to do what you always wanted to but couldn't.)

Parents

• List the expectations you have for your son. Be honest about why you hold these and think of the possible positive and negative consequences for him of each one.

• Think about sports, music, art, school, career, hobbies and leisure, and whether your expectations of your child are high, medium or low for each one. If there are lots of "highs," rethink your expectations.

• Ask him whether he agrees with your goals and whether he feels he can, or knows how to, meet them.

• Look at whether your short-term academic expectations are realistic, and how you will feel if he fails to meet them.

Teachers

• Boys need high, but achievable, short-term goals. Ensure that your personal goals and school goals don't impose undue pressure on your students.

• Help boys to define their own expectations. Step in only if they have misjudged things seriously, either positively or negatively.

92 What you expect is what you get

"Time for school in ten minutes. Remember what you need and I'll see you at the front door at a quarter to." For older boys, this is a far more helpful and positive approach than "You have only ten minutes. Have you got your homework? Have you brushed your teeth? Don't forget your folder, and don't be late like yesterday!"

Boys who feel trusted by an adult feel proud of that trust and work at keeping it. Research consistently shows that high expectations produce good results, and low expectations produce poor ones—what you expect is what you get. "What you expect" in this case is your perception of your child's personality and behavior. "What you get" is the behavior you expect. So if you ask a boy to do something in a way that assumes and expects that he will, you are more likely to get the result you want. The reverse is also true: When you imply that he won't cooperate or succeed at something, he probably won't.

Parents

- Remain positive: Notice, constantly, the things that he does right. If he fails to do something, restate your request or expectation. Don't berate him for his omission.

- Stop predicting or assuming poor performance or behavior with phrases such as "I suppose you'll fail this test, too" or even "You will be good, won't you?"

- Avoid sticking labels on him, especially negative ones such as "naughty," "thief," "liar" and "bad." Give him hope and faith in himself.

Teachers

- Have appropriate and realistic expectations for the content of students' work and high expectations for quality of presentation and meeting deadlines.

- Many boys find it hard to produce neat work, but they won't develop this skill if their gender becomes an excuse. Computers can help improve the look of a boy's work and encourage him to see himself as capable of high standards.

- Encourage reflection. This should be demonstrated in written work and class discussion. With this expectation, boys are more likely to develop this important ability.

93 Watch your words

Words have enormous power. What parents and teachers say, and how they say it, can have enormous impact. Boys are as susceptible to hurtful words and criticism as girls, despite any pretense they make of being tough and immune to insult.

Without realizing it, we can say things that humiliate boys and damage their self-belief and self-respect. Fathers and father figures, especially, are prone to engage in playful, teasing banter with their sons that includes threats, sarcasm and insult. They do this partly because they are uncomfortable with straightforward praise and intimacy and partly because it makes them feel powerful and superior. However, vulnerable boys will never be certain that no criticism was intended.

If we want relationships with boys that help them to feel loved and cared for, we must make fewer comments and reprimands that undermine them, even in jest.

Parents

- Verbal teasing is a form of manipulation that should be used carefully and sparingly.

- Give plenty of praise and kind words. These won't lead to pride if we teach that "good at" means "different from" in abilities, not "better than."

- Be aware that when we put our children down, it can be a defense mechanism to protect our own sense of inadequacy.

- Comments such as "I can't take you anywhere," "I don't care what you think," "What's so good about that?", "You'll probably end up in prison," and "You'll never learn" will systematically destroy a boy's self-esteem and self-belief.

Teachers

- Be positive at all times. Sparring with a confident boy may be acceptable for him but may frighten another boy into silence.

- Research has shown that confident five-year-olds entering school can become unsure of themselves and develop "learned helplessness" when subjected to constant criticism and negative comments about their work and play.

- Boys generally prefer to be active and doing, have trouble listening and are less sophisticated at managing social encounters and group discussion than girls. Tailor your comments accordingly.

94 Loosen the straitjacket

Why are you always so lazy and messy? Why can't you be neat like your sister? She just puts her things away with no arguments. You're just like your father!

Straitjackets are statements about a person that lock him into a role and deny him any possibility of being different. "You always . . . ," "You are just like . . . ," "You will never . . ." are typical examples. Everyone develops and changes throughout their lives. It is unfair in the extreme to get fixed ideas about anyone, especially a child. Straitjackets can encourage a boy to become whatever you tell him he is, because he'll give up trying to be different.

Straitjackets come in two forms:

1. labels, which describe what a boy is and what he is not: "You are a moron, an idiot," "You'll never be any good at school," "Why don't you ever tell the truth or finish anything?"
2. comparisons, which measure a boy against someone more favored: "Ahmed's much more reliable than you."

Parents

• Try to move from "Why?" questions to "I" statements.

• "Why are you . . . ?" accusations are the most insulting, because a boy is forced to acknowledge your description in order to defend himself. "I see you as . . . when . . ." is more acceptable. It puts the emphasis firmly on your feelings, is specific about the circumstances and makes clear that he's not always like that.

• Make a mental or written note of the things your son "always" does, then be on the look-out for breaks in the pattern, when he behaves contrary to expectation.

• Take "always" and "never" out of your vocabulary.

Teachers

• Don't compare. When you find yourself teaching another child from the same family, don't mention the talents or failings of one to the other.

• Try a class activity in which your students discuss different types of insults and the impact they have. Consider blame, sarcasm and ridicule. Get them to practice using "I" statements instead.

• Unbuckle your own straitjacket. Teachers can be as guilty as parents of failing to revise their opinions about individual personalities in the face of contrary evidence.

95 Model respect for women

The best thing a father or father figure can do for the children in his care is to show love and respect for their mother. This reinforces her authority, strengthens the children's respect for her and helps them feel secure in themselves and within the family. Most important, it also models respect for all women.

Boys will do better and do themselves justice if they distance themselves from macho culture, which tends to reject anything vaguely female or associated with women as weak and inferior.

If we want to encourage boys to develop a more caring image of masculinity, we must show respect for women, including female teachers, and the particular strengths and qualities that women possess. Verbal or physical abuse and violence toward women, especially a boy's mother, is often the single most damaging factor to a boy's self-esteem, mental health and future success in life.

Parents

• Earn his respect. If you don't treat others, including absent parents, with due respect, he may lose his respect for you.

• Be careful about the tone and content of your casual remarks when watching movies or television. A lot of swearing, for example, implies disrespect for others.

• Mothers, don't let your son walk all over you. Boys won't learn to respect women if you don't respect yourself. Taking time for yourself and maintaining house rules to protect your interests are marks of self-respect.

Teachers

• Discuss with colleagues whether you could introduce a sexual harassment policy in your school, if you don't have one already. Girls should, of course, be prepared to treat boys with the same respect they may wish to receive in return.

• Gender awareness and equality of respect should apply throughout the school and in every lesson.

96 Don't swamp him with your success

My dad was a successful self-made man. He did it all on his own and he never let us forget it. He did really well, flashed his money around, and I had no idea how I was going to live up to him, which is what he expected. I was terrified when I left school and the future stared me in the face.

It's surprising how many boys follow in their successful mother's or father's footsteps and do as well, if not better, in the same career. But for every success story, there will be another in which the son gives up because he feels he can't compete. The danger comes when a parent's sense of self-worth is based on his or her success. When you flaunt your own success, because you see it as the only way to gain acceptability, you force your values and your view of the world onto your son. He may have different attitudes and interests.

Parents

- Handle your success with modesty and sensitivity. Show that you regard it as a result of your interest, commitment and hard work, not your genius—and keep it as your thing, not his.

- Your success will be evident even if you don't blow your own horn. You'll still be a good role model.

- Don't try to excel at every activity. Doing something well enough, without comment, and showing that you sometimes fail is a useful example for your son.

- Two successful parents operating in different fields make it harder for a boy to find his own niche, so that it is even more important to value the things he likes and does well.

Teachers

- When a boy is struggling with something he finds difficult, it won't help him to show how easy it is by racing through a repeated explanation.

- Underachieving boys may not feel capable of following in your footsteps (or those of any other role model). Explain carefully, stage by stage, how you reached your present position to show it's a manageable goal.

97 You bring about what you fear

My dad was terrified I'd get into drugs. He never trusted me.
He checked my things, nosed around into where I went and
who with. He spied on me constantly. I got so fed up that I
went out more and got in with a crowd that was into drugs.

There's a frightening, almost magnetic, force that seems to
operate alongside our fears: The more we want something
for our sons, or fear that they will or won't do something,
the more we seem to bring about what we *don't* want by our
overconcerned behavior, which they then react to. If we're
afraid a boy's going to grow up naughty, we use harsher
punishments, which may encourage him to rebel. If we ban
candy and cookies from the house, he'll buy them and
binge when he can. If we force him to practice his music
because he has the talent to excel, he'll lose his love of it
and give up.

The common threads are trust and power. If we have little
trust, and we use our power inappropriately to manage our
fears, we are more likely to turn them into a reality.

Parents

• Identify your fears and think about whether you handle these in a way that makes them self-fulfilling.

• Try to get your fears into perspective. Discuss with someone else how real they are, how important it is that your son achieves in the way you wish him to and, if the worst happened, whether it really would be that terrible.

• Give him as much scope as possible to take care of himself, within guidelines you set.

• Reward the behavior you want to see rather than punishing lapses.

Teachers

• Identify your fears for a particularly difficult class, individual or relationship with a colleague. You may fear being seen as incompetent, disorganized, too harsh and so on. Reflect on your responses and try to change the ones you don't like.

• Think about the fears of the other person or people you have just identified and how these might interplay with your own.

• Suggest that boys in your class be open about their own fears, in and outside school. They may fear coming across as weak or nerdy. Ask how this colors their reactions in life.

98 The more you use it, the more you lose it

I saw a young boy getting bored while his mother talked with a friend on the sidewalk. He decided to run away toward the road, so his mother grabbed him, dragged him back, hit him and resumed her conversation. He did the same again, twice, and so did she. The third time, he ran out into the road and she hit him harder, several times. The more she hit, the more he chose to flout her authority.

There is an important lesson to learn about power, which is that the more you use it, the more you lose it. When power is used, or misused, frequently, it doesn't stop children from doing something but incites them to challenge it further. Perhaps children see people with an overreliance on power as weak underneath, and they exploit this weakness. More likely, they resent their inferior skills and being taken advantage of. Being neither understood nor treated with the respect they deserve, they express their frustration in the only way they can.

Parents

- Hitting is not the only power tactic parents use. They use threats, bribes, harsh punishments and elaborate reasoning to get their way. Children watch and learn these tactics, too.

- We remain authoritative not by being authoritarian but by continuing to guide, influence, set boundaries for decisions and, sometimes, direct when necessary.

Teachers

- Boys are often less compliant than girls and have the confidence to argue and make their point if they feel unfairly treated. If you fail to listen, you could lose in the long term.

- Lessening your control will not necessarily undermine your authority. Put boys more in charge of their own learning, allow them to evaluate their own and each others' work under your guidance, and the potential for destructive, power-based dynamics will be reduced to a minimum.

99 Let him grow wings

Independence is a vital and exciting part of growing up for boys. Gaining in competence; meeting challenges and overcoming obstacles; experimenting with risks and different ways of doing things; gaining more control over what happens to him and learning to set his own boundaries are all essential for a boy to become an independent and responsible adult.

Unfortunately, the world outside the home is seen as an increasingly dangerous place. Naturally, parents are worried about allowing children to play and travel without adult supervision. Instead of encouraging children to go off on their own and experiment, gradually giving them more freedom, they tend to supervise, chaperone, constrain and contain them. They drive children around, even a couple blocks, and discourage them from playing even in the front yard, let alone in the street or park. Keeping children safely indoors enables parents to relax. To add virtue to self-interest, they believe that they are doing the best for their child. But learning to handle risk and cope with the unknown increases confidence and is an important life skill. Boys need to grow wings and learn to use them.

Parents

• Opportunities to be on his own give him the chance to test himself. Without them, he'll find it harder to establish his identity, develop self-esteem and adjust socially by finding out how to behave in and belong to bigger groups.

• Increase his freedom outside the home gradually. At first he should stay with older siblings or within the safety of a trustworthy group.

• Less socially minded boys can satisfy their desire for independence by traveling on local buses for fun, learning to use maps and schedules.

Teachers

• Discourage parents from coming to peek at their child through the fence at recess. If he sees them, he'll feel tied down rather than loved.

• Some children learn to use their wings by trying out different ways of working. Treat this respectfully and be as flexible as possible.

• Classwork in subjects such as math or geography can involve the use of bus and train schedules, which will enhance self-management skills.

100 Prove your commitment

Inner strength is built on commitment. Children need to feel they have the commitment of at least one significant adult in order to grow up happy, confident, secure and resilient, and strong enough within themselves to be able to give to others. Birth parents are not the only ones who can offer this. A child who is able to commit to learning and friendships despite personal problems usually mentions the commitment of someone who spent time with him, showed interest in the things he did, accepted him as he was and, crucially, was reliable and there for him when he needed support.

Your commitment will help your son to have the confidence to think well of and for himself; to be in a minority of one and take any flak, yet be flexible enough to compromise on issues of lesser importance. He'll have the strength to hear constructive criticism and not experience every challenge as a personal slight. He'll have enough curiosity to explore and think ahead so that he gains the necessary foresight, power and willpower to determine his future and not be a victim. His self-esteem, happiness and confidence may depend on it.

Parents

• You can prove your commitment in many ways: being interested, cherishing, caring, keeping him safe, offering support, making his birthday special and helping him to make sense of his world.

• Showing that you think about him when he's not there is important, too. For example, "I bought your favorite cookies at the store today."

• Step-parents and new partners have to work harder at commitment, particularly when a boy has already been let down.

• Behaving in a consistent way and keeping promises to call, write or visit are essential ways to show commitment.

Teachers

• Be aware that when a boy is going through a tough time personally, especially when he loses a parent or parent figure through death, illness or separation, he will need a clear commitment from someone like you—even though he may doubt and test it.

• Show your commitment through patience, tolerance and problem-solving with him when he does not behave and achieve as he used to. There may be simple, practical solutions if you look carefully.

• Never give up on a child. He may give up on himself, but it is your professional and personal responsibility to continue to offer him hope.

Further Reading . . .

Declaire, Joan, et al. *Raising an Emotionally Intelligent Child* (Fireside, 1998)

Greenspan, Stanley I., M.D., and Jaqueline Salmon. *Playground Politics: Understanding the Emotional Life of the School-Age Child* (Perseus Publishing, 1994)

Gurian, Michael, et al. *The Prince and the King: Healing the Father-Son Wound, a Guided Journey of Initiation* (J. P. Tarcher, 1993)

Hartley-Brewer, Elizabeth. *Raising Confident Girls: 100 Tips for Parents and Teachers* (Fisher Books, 2000)

Kindlon, Daniel J., and Michael Thompson. *Raising Cain: Protecting the Emotional Life of Boys* (Ballantine Books, 2000)

Kurcinka, Mary Sheedy. *Kids, Parents, and Power Struggles: Winning for a Lifetime* (HarperCollins, 2000)

Nagy, Allen, et al. *How to Raise Your Child's Emotional Intelligence: 101 Ways to Bring Out the Best in Your Children and Yourself* (Heartfelt Publications, 1999)

Newmark, Gerald, Ph.D. *How to Raise Emotionally Healthy Children: Meeting the Five Critical Needs of Children . . . and Parents too!* (Newmark Management Institute, 1999)

Paul, Henry A. *When Kids Are Mad, Not Bad: A Guide to Recognizing and Handling Your Child's Anger* (Berkley Publishing Group, 1999)

Seligman, Martin E. P., et al. *The Optimistic Child* (HarperPerennial Library, 1996)

Shapiro, Lawrence E. *How to Raise a Child With a High EQ: A Parent's Guide to Emotional Intelligence* (HarperCollins, 1998)